WITHIN REACH

Your Journey to Being
Likable, Hirable,
and Mostly Sane

*A Roadmap for Overthinking
Ambitious People*

JOHN KUNDLY
@reachwithjohn

ISBN: 979-8-9937343-0-9

First Edition: 2026
Printed in the United States of America

*For everyone who thinks the
life they want is too far away:*

*It's closer than you think!
It's within reach.*

CONTENTS

FOREWORD

by Joe Manganiello

I met John at the gym.

I'd seen him there day after day, until finally we were working out on adjacent equipment and he said hi. We got to talking, and right away, I got a good feeling about him. He was grounded and friendly in ways that you don't find very often in Los Angeles.

He, like me, had moved out west from a blue-collar town to pursue his dreams. He hailed from Youngstown, Ohio, a short 45-minute drive from the neighborhood where I grew up in Pittsburgh. People from that part of the world share an ethos—there truly is something "in the water."

I could tell immediately—just by seeing him at that gym every day—that John understood something most people don't: talent can be debated, explained away, and judged by committees...but discipline and hard work can't. You either showed up or you didn't. You either put in the reps or you didn't. And John showed up.

That's what you're going to feel in these pages.

Within Reach isn't a book about getting lucky, or being born with some rare gift, or finding the perfect moment to start. It's about learning to handle the things that are actually in your control—your effort, your habits, your choices, your character—and using them to build a life you can be proud of. Not a life that looks good online. A life that holds up under pressure.

John has always relished the responsibility of that.

He was also very generous with his time. When he heard I was trying to get into great shape for my next role, he offered to put together a diet and workout program for me—free of charge. At that point, I had been living in Los Angeles for eight years, and I had forgotten what it was like to have someone offer to do something for you without wanting something in return. John reminded me of home.

I took him up on his offer, and out of respect for his effort, I followed his directions to a T.

We became fast friends. I realized very quickly that he was one of those people who says what he means and does what he says. If I ever needed John, I knew I could count on him—and vice versa. I served as a member of John's wedding party and watched him grow into a fantastic husband and father. Through dark times and fun times, he's been there for me like a rock, with grounded words that don't come from theory... they come from lived experience.

And here's the part I think matters most about this book: John doesn't just "believe" in growth. He knows how to build it.

I respect him for his ability to pivot when life sends something difficult. He's incredibly intelligent and has always found another ladder to jump to—and managed to climb his way up it. He has never let anything get in the way of his desire to grow, and he's never let his ego come before the things he values most in life.

That's what makes *Within Reach* different. A lot of books will hype you up for an hour and leave you the same. This one is built like John is built: disciplined, practical, and honest. It's a playbook for people who want to move—really move—without pretending it's easy. It gives you language for what you're feeling, frameworks for what to do next, and reminders to keep going even when nobody is clapping yet.

If you're reading this and you feel stuck, or overwhelmed, or behind—if you're the kind of person who has big goals but a mind that can talk you out of taking the next step—this book is for you. Read it like you'd train with John. Show up. Take the first rep seriously. Follow the program. Trust the process.

Because the truth is: the life you want isn't reserved for a special group of people. It's closer than you think. It's within reach.

There are a handful of people I would trust with my innermost thoughts and my family's well-being, and John is most certainly one of them. When he calls, I answer. When he speaks, I listen.

Now, it's your turn.

The Unintentional Beginning of Everything Intentional

First off, thank you. Seriously. The fact that you've made it this far means you've read the title, survived the table of contents, and somehow decided *this* was still worth your time. I'm humbled. Truly. I never planned to write a book. In fact, I distinctly remember saying something along the lines of "I could never write a book."

People who know me usually start with the same shocked question: "Wait... You wrote a book?" They say it with that mix of disbelief and laughter usually reserved for toddlers explaining quantum physics. After I give them my standard smart-aleck answer, they hit me with the real question: "But why?"

The short answer: I felt led to write it. The long answer: I couldn't *not* write it. That actually wasn't much longer. Let me try again: I wrote *Within Reach* for the people who feel like I used to—who think that life should be *more than it is.* For the ones who know they're capable of more but can't quite see the path. For the ambitious overthinkers who spend so much time planning their potential that they forget to live it.

If you've ever felt stuck, disconnected from your purpose, or haunted by that tiny voice whispering "You're not enough!", this book is for you. If your life is already perfect, stress-free, and everything you've ever dreamed of...well, congrats! Also, my contact info is in the back. I need to know your secret. Like, yesterday.

What You Can Expect

Here's what this isn't: a self-help book. Here's what it is: a *success manual* disguised as comedy, psychology, and Sunday-morning conviction. It's equal parts faith, neuroscience, storytelling, and "Wait, did he really just say that?"

Throughout *Within Reach*, one truth quietly anchors every story, framework, and toolkit: you're not as far away from "more" as you think you are. The version of you that's confident, peaceful, magnetic, and purposeful isn't some upgraded prototype waiting years down the line, it's already built in right now. What you've been calling "self-doubt" is usually just misalignment. What you've been calling "waiting on God" is often Him waiting on you to get still enough to listen.

Each chapter peels back a layer of ego, fear, overthinking, and performance. Rather than needing to add more, you'll realize that being likable, hirable, and mostly sane is about *becoming lighter.* The real science of success is found in harmony, not the hustle. When faith, psychology, and a bit of humor finally sync up, you realize the truth that's been whispering all along: everything you've been praying for is already within reach.

Inside this book, you'll find real, practical tools to help you:

- Build unshakable confidence (even when your brain is screaming otherwise).
- Communicate like a leader who actually gets invited back to the meeting.
- Understand the psychology of likability, influence, and resilience.
- Finally be able to start closing the gap between who you are and who you're meant to be.

Every chapter pairs stories (usually ones where I messed up spectacularly) with a framework or toolkit that will help you apply the lesson to your own life. Think of the chapters as being like your favorite Netflix show that combines drama and documentary and makes you say, "How did we end up here?"

How to Get the Most Out of This Book

Don't just read this book, *train with it.* Highlight it like it owes you money. Dog-ear the pages like you're claiming land. Argue with me in the margins if you must. (I won't hear you, but somewhere in Heaven, an angel will nod in solidarity.)

Every chapter ends with a Within Reach Toolkit. That's the part where reading stops and *doing* begins. Don't skip it! You need to make a conscious effort to move to the "doing" stage, because unfortunately, although reading about doing something feels dangerously similar to actually doing it, it's not the same thing. It's a psychological prank, a cognitive April Fool's Day that happens 365 days a year. Neuroscientists call the phenomenon mental substitution, and it's when your brain confuses planning for progress—you make a plan and your brain fires off dopamine and tells you something like "Great job, champ! We nailed it!" even though you haven't done a single thing except make bullet points in your Notes app. It's the spiritual equivalent of praying for change but never leaving the couch. (Yes, God loves you. Yes, He also expects you to stand up occasionally.)

This is why actually *using* the Within Reach Toolkit is nonnegotiable. It's the antidote to the magic trick of mental substitution, the difference between *knowing* and *becoming.* Between "I should" and "I did." In short, while reading gives you the blueprint, the toolkit hands you the hammer.

When you apply what you read—even messily, even imperfectly—you start building the version of you that's been tugging at your spirit for years. But in order for that version to actually show up, you need to *act* on it, not just think about it.

If you want to go deeper, I built a full workbook to help you push past the highlight-and-hope phase. It's where the real breakthroughs happen—the kind you can feel and measure, the kind when people start asking you, "Hey, what changed?"

Spoiler: You did.

If you treat this like a book, sure, you'll get some laughs and a few aha moments. But if you treat it like a *mirror*, a tool that will allow you to see yourself clearly, then you'll walk away with something far more powerful: growth and momentum. The distance between who you are and who you want to be isn't a canyon, it's a *reach.* A decision. A moment of courage repeated enough times to change your trajectory. That's why this book is called *Within Reach.* Because it is.

So buckle up, because it's going to be a bumpy ride! Not like hit-a-pothole-with-no-suspension bumpy, but Six-Flags-screaming-your-lungs-out-but-kinda-loving-it bumpy. There will be twists, drops, and probably a few moments when you wonder aloud, "What did I sign up for?" If you stick with it, though, you'll realize something that took me years to understand: you were never as far away from your purpose as you thought. You were always closer than you believed. You were always *within reach.*

CHAPTER 1

Own Your 14:24

You're hungry. Not the kind of hungry that makes you order DoorDash at midnight, but the feed-my-soul-kind of hungry, the kind that whispers, "I know I'm built for more." That's good news! Because everything from this point forward requires the version of you that shows up on purpose, not by accident.

Your breakthrough won't come from big, dramatic moments—it's going to come from small, invisible ones. The decisions made when no one is clapping, posting, or handing out trophies. The quiet stuff. The unsexy stuff. And look, I know the market is saturated with the "1% better" concept. But before you roll your eyes, let me make it practical. Like, math-on-a-napkin practical:

1% of your day is 864 seconds. That's 14 minutes and 24 seconds.

That 1% isn't a life overhaul. It's not a "new you" campaign with a logo. It's not a dramatic comeback story with background music and a rain scene. It just points this out: if you can carve out 14 minutes and 24 seconds in your day, you can get 1% better. So, what are you going to do with your 14:24?

While God hides transformation in repetition, neuroscience hides mastery in micro-moves. Life hides momentum in tiny yeses. That's why we're going to begin where every great transformation actually starts, which is to say long before any results are visible.

First, the bad news: there is no such thing as overnight success. Now for the good news! God, psychology, and mathematics all agree on one thing: small doesn't mean insignificant, it means compounded. Think about how compound interest builds up over time—rather than looking for fireworks, look for patterns and nudges. Look for that quiet conviction that says, "I can do this. Even if nobody sees me doing it."

That's the 1% nobody sees. And now it has a timestamp: 14 minutes and 24 seconds, the daily deposit that builds the life you keep praying for.

All of that said, I need to confess that I'm a recovering "overnight success" addict. You know the type: the person who sees someone post their new Ferrari pic or their "Just promoted to CEO!" selfie and immediately thinks, *Wow. Must be nice!* As if success and enlightenment could be Prime-delivered overnight.

I used to believe life was a series of big breaks and inspirational montages...but then I met reality. Reality doesn't montage, it meanders and delays. It loops you endlessly through the same unglamorous steps, until you start questioning your life choices and googling, "Is perseverance supposed to feel this dumb?" And yet, that's where the secret starts: the part no one spotlights, the grind people stop paying attention to, the in-between that shapes everything that comes after.

Then years later, everyone notices your success and says, "Man, you came out of nowhere!" But I didn't come out of nowhere, and you won't, either. I came out of consistency. Out of small reps. Out of a daily choice to protect a small slice of time and do something that mattered more than what was easy.

That's the 1% nobody sees. That's the 14:24 nobody protects.

The Myth of the Big Moment

We love to romanticize transformation—Hollywood sells us before-and-after shots like they're miracle products. The "before" is tragic, broke, heartbroken, and eating cold pizza over a sink. The "after" is someone suddenly glowing like they discovered an amazing skincare routine and emotional stability in the same week.

But real change isn't cinematic, it's domestic. It's washing the same dish over and over again because you realize you suck at washing dishes and growth doesn't come with a chore exemption.

The things that look small, boring, invisible, or repetitive are actually the roots of the life everyone else will later call "impressive." That's what I mean by the 1%: the stuff nobody sees is about micro-moves and tiny pivots that compound into massive shifts. I'm talking about the text you don't send out of pride and the apology you do send out of grace. That's the 1%. It's doing the workout when you'd rather doomscroll and the prayer when you're too tired to feel holy. It's not sexy or shareable, but it does compound. Slowly. Invisibly. Faithfully.

And here's the part people skip: the 1% isn't a vibe, it's a block of time. It's 14 minutes and 24 seconds where you tell your day, "You don't own me. I'm choosing on purpose."

Of course, we all want the reward without the repetition. But God's economy is compound interest, not lottery tickets, and when you meet someone who "made it," you're just seeing the interest phase. Meanwhile, they've been quietly depositing invisible effort coins for years into the account called Consistent Obedience.

One of my favorite examples of someone who made his deposits and kept on making them is my friend Eric, a.k.a. the "overnight" success story that actually took ten years.

Eric started a podcast in his garage in 2013. For seven years, nobody listened. He had single-digit Spotify stats, one of whom was his mom. He was one mic check away from quitting and drowning in thoughts of *Maybe I'm just not meant to make this work...* Then one random episode blew up because his guest, a local chef, went viral for ranting about sourdough starters.

Overnight, Eric hit two million downloads. Everyone called it fate. Eric called it finally.

His story is an excellent illustration of why invisible consistency is so hard and why most people quit right before "finally" begins. "Finally" isn't magic, it's math. It's what happens when you keep protecting your 14:24 long enough for the world to catch up to what God has been building in you.

The Psychology of Invisible Effort

There's a gem in behavioral science known as the progress principle. It says we feel happiest when we sense we're moving forward, even slightly. But our brains are wired for fireworks, not flickers, and so patience feels painful. In short, dopamine loves drama, and that leads us to mistake *visible* progress for *real* progress. Except neurons fire before muscles flex, which is to say change happens in the wiring before it happens in the world. Our brains literally build new roads while we're stuck in traffic thinking nothing's happening.

The 1% isn't loud or glamorous, but it is the quiet neurological construction zone called "becoming." Once you grasp the psychology behind that (sometimes uncomfortable) truth, you'll start seeing how it transforms your own habits. In finance, your money makes money while you sleep; in life, your habits do the same thing. Each rep earns psychological interest until discipline automates itself. That's when "I have to" becomes "I just do."

Here's why the 14:24 matters: because it lowers the entry fee. You don't need an hour. You don't need a perfect schedule. You don't need a motivational song and a fresh notebook and a "Monday reset." You need **14 minutes and 24 seconds,** the smallest daily deposit that still counts as "I showed up."

Once you hit that stage, what used to be an effort becomes your identity. Until then, remember that you're not tired, you're under-compounded. And especially remember that the beauty of compounding is that it doesn't require dramatic beginnings, just small, faithful ones.

I once mentored a student who went on to epitomize the progress principle. She said, "I want to write a book, but I never have time."

I said, "Cool. Give me 14 minutes and 24 seconds."

She looked at me like I'd offered her a coloring book and a crayon, but she did it. Most days, she wrote longer once she'd gotten started, and those 14 minutes turned into 40, then 400. Six months later, she'd written 40,000 words. Her first draft wasn't perfect, but you know what's better than perfect? *Done.* Because the Holy Spirit can't edit what you never start.

Speaking of starting without seeing results immediately, let's talk about how hilariously sneaky progress can be. Because it is hilarious. You grind for years, and then one Tuesday someone says, "Hey, you seem different." And you spiral into an identity crisis and think, *Wait, so it worked? When did that happen?!*

Growth breaks in like a thief in the night, right after you stopped checking the locks. You don't notice it until it's standing in your living room saying, "Surprise! I was happening all along." Which seems counterintuitive, because our brains crave novelty, not monotony. But monotony is how we rewire our default settings. Consistency feels boring only because it's working in the background.

And the daily 14:24? That's monotony with purpose. That's boring... on assignment.

The Emotional Tax of the Long Game

Nobody talks about how boring discipline is. Motivation is loud; discipline is beige. Tired beige sometimes, uninspired beige other times. Discipline means you get things done even when your motivation's hiding under a weighted blanket muttering, "Not today!"

Discipline doesn't care about your mood—it's built on commitment, not chemistry. If you wait to feel "ready," you'll wait forever, so you have to start when you're *not* ready. Your feelings will catch up. The brain learns from repetition, not inspiration, and habits get ingrained through friction, not hype. Boredom is a sign you're doing it right. It can also be a sign that you're on exactly the right path.

And I know what you're thinking: *Okay, John, but I don't have time.* No, what you don't have is protected time. Most of us can find 15 minutes. We just spend it accidentally. We lose it to scrolling. To spiraling. To "one more thing." We donate it to everybody else's agenda. But 14:24 isn't about more time, it's about a new standard: I protect one small slice of my day like my future depends on it, because it does.

I've met the epitome of this truth in the form of a barista named Jordan who worked near my old office. Every morning, same vibe: cheerful, patient, latte art like the Mona Lisa. Turned out, he was saving every tip to fund his chemistry degree.

Now, nine years later, he's a research scientist developing biodegradable plastics. Everyone calls him brilliant. He just smiles and says, "Persistence looks a lot like boredom." Nobody else saw a scientist disguised as a barista who spent day after day turning caffeine into compound success.

So, if you're like most people, you need to reframe your thoughts around boredom. And around frustration, too, because if boredom doesn't stop you, frustration might. After all, we now live in an era where the algorithm rewards urgency. We crave instant likes and instant validation, and so we wind up with instant frustration that leads to burnout. When progress lags, we assume everything is broken.

But progress is like slow Wi-Fi that *is* still buffering, just not at your preferred speed. Faith is staying logged in even when the screen freezes. Our current world doesn't have a failure problem, we have a frustration tolerance problem: we mistake delay for denial. That is unfortunately where identity starts shaping everything, causing us to get stuck in the identity loop as well as the comparison trap.

The identity loop happens because behavior creates identity and identity reinforces behavior. The hard truth is that you can't think your way into confidence, so the alternative is to act confident until your brain stops filing complaints. Every time you follow through—even if it's just for 14:24—you send a signal to yourself that says, "I can trust myself." That self-trust is the invisible 1%.

Identity also directly affects the comparison trap, a.k.a. the comparison game. That's a game best not played—comparison drains momentum because it tricks our brain into thinking we're behind, when really, we're just in a different chapter. Some of those chapters can take years to bloom.

Micro Wins, Macro Impact

One way to escape the comparison trap is to celebrate effort, not outcome. Didn't finish the marathon? You still trained for it. Didn't get the job? You still built interview muscle. Didn't go viral? You still built resilience. The reward isn't the result, it's the resilience you built getting there. It's the 1% nobody sees.

Sometimes the 1% shows up in the most unexpected leadership moments. I saw that happen with a local high school gym teacher named Mr. Reynolds. He ran a 5K every year, and he always finished dead last on purpose. He'd make sure he was at the back of the pack to cheer on the students who wanted to quit. When asked why, he said, "Because my win is watching you finish." That's the 1%, and that's also quiet leadership: effort that doesn't trend but transforms.

But what about when the 1% feels absolutely pointless? The plateau, the purgatory between starting and success, is where enthusiasm dies and consistency gets tested. It's the part nobody puts on Instagram. It's also the part that builds you.

Growth is like a staircase with missing steps, and sometimes you just have to levitate emotionally until the next one appears. Luckily, here's where science backs your resilience. Patience is neurochemical maturity: every time you delay gratification, your prefrontal cortex overrides your amygdala. You're literally rewiring your emotional resilience. Each time you wait and don't quit, you upgrade your firmware. That's growth you can't post about, but one that you can and need to live by. Eventually, all that invisible rewiring creates something powerful: momentum.

Momentum isn't visible at first because it's building inside you—it's the energy that accumulates between action and outcome. That's why you can grind for years...and then suddenly everything accelerates. It's not luck, it's lag! Momentum arrives like a delayed delivery from Heaven. You placed the order years ago; it's just finally shipping.

When momentum *does* ship, the freedom you gain looks a lot like what my friend Leo wound up having. During the pandemic, he started running because he needed control. At first, he could barely make a mile, but still, he posted every run on Strava, not for clout, but for accountability. Three years later, he ran a marathon. He finished mid-pack, but at Mile 25, he cried. Because no one was watching and he was doing it anyway. *That's* freedom: effort divorced from audience.

Which leads to the emotional side of quiet success. People will overlook you while you're building and doubt you while you're planting. They'll probably call you "lucky" when it blooms. And that's just fine, because you'll know the truth: the unseen part, the long part, the sacred grind. The 1% nobody sees.

You'll know that when the light finally finds you, it won't be luck. It'll be your consistency catching up to God's timing...one protected 14:24 at a time.

WITHIN REACH TOOLKIT
The 1% GPS

If you keep doing what nobody sees, one day you'll become what everybody notices. And you'll know that success didn't happen overnight, it happened because you had faith and discipline and you did the 1% nobody saw.

Here's how to make sure your newfound consistency sticks:

1. Lower the bar! Progress hates perfectionism.
2. Track effort, not outcome.
3. Be boring on purpose. Discipline is glamorous in hindsight.

4. Detach from the scoreboard. It's about alignment, not attention.
5. Repeat until it feels natural. Then repeat again.

Progress feels awkward because you're building it up privately; you're laying the foundation everyone else will one day stand upon. That foundation becomes even more powerful when you use it intentionally. And now with the math in your hands, you can stop wondering what 1% requires: **it requires 14 minutes and 24 seconds.** If you can find 15 minutes in your day, you can get 1% better.

So again, the question that changes everything: what will you do with your 14:24? You're about to lay down your first cornerstone!

Step 1: Recalibrate. Audit energy, not results.

Ask yourself weekly:

- What gave me energy?
- What drained me?
- What was I avoiding but then I felt better once I did it?

Your energy is a compass. Track patterns, not perfection.

Step 2: Reroute. Translate Plateaus into Practice.

When progress stalls, ask yourself, "What's still working that I'm not celebrating?" Small wins fuel endurance. Plateaus are proof you're carrying heavier weight.

Step 3: Refuel. Run on gratitude and micro-impact.

Each night, jot down three things:

1. One thing that made me proud.
2. One person I encouraged.
3. One thing I learned about myself.

Gratitude is performance fuel disguised as perspective.

Step 4: Repeat. Consistency is a language.

1. Do the rep.
2. Do it again.

3. Do it especially when no one's watching.

Motion is the language of purpose. Fluency comes with repetition.

Bonus Rule: Ignore the algorithm of comparison.

Your timeline isn't your life's timeline! The algorithm rewards noise; life rewards alignment. If you're building slowly, you're building strong.

The 14:24 Doorway

Hopefully by now you're on board with being consistent and doing what nobody sees day in and day out. Here's the thing, though: Consistency has a twin brother, and he's called Work. And that's where most people quietly bow out, because once the inspiration fades, what's left is effort—the sweat, the silence, the grind of not-yet.

The space between "I want it" and "I'm willing to work for it" is the gap where discipline meets doubt and shortcuts start whispering sweet nothings like, "Psst! There's an easier way!" But God doesn't build character in shortcuts, He builds it in the stretch. He's not trying to get you there faster, He's trying to make sure you can stay there once you arrive.

So, protect your 14:24. Not because it's a cute concept, but because it's the daily proof that you're becoming who you said you were.

And the 1% nobody sees? That's where it all starts.

CHAPTER 2

The Myth of the Shortcut

We all love a good shortcut story: the "I just posted one video and blew up overnight!" story, the "I met one person and suddenly everything changed!" story, the "I manifested it in a week and now I have brand deals and a gluten-free sense of purpose!" story. We eat those stories like candy. But here's the thing about shortcuts: they always start as blessings and end as detours. Why? Because what looks like a faster way *around* the work is usually just a longer way *back* to it.

I used to think I could out-hustle the whole process—that if I read enough, strategized enough, outworked enough, I could skip the messy middle, the awkward learning curve where confidence is low and caffeine intake is high. But every time I tried to skip it, life handed me a humble pie with extra "Told you so!" filling. Turns out, God's not in the business of skipping steps. He's in the business of strengthening legs.

But of course, there's a reason why our brains crave shortcuts. Psychologists call it cognitive efficiency. It's the brain's desire to conserve energy and avoid unnecessary effort, and it explains why we look for the Easy button and why fad diets exist. In short, our brains hate friction. But faith? Faith is built *in* friction.

To be fair to ourselves, though, shortcuts promise control, and that's incredibly tempting. Shortcuts whisper, "You can get the reward without the resistance." But the resistance is the whole point—it's what forms endurance, identity, and trust. Without resistance, strength is an illusion. Every shortcut is really just a skipped lesson disguised as an opportunity. And God, in His divine patience, will lovingly reassign us the same lesson until we pass the test. Same pattern; different players. New outfit; same curriculum. Some roads are long not because God's cruel, but because He's kind enough *not* to let us arrive unprepared.

Why We Keep Looking for Quick Fixes

Humans are wired for efficiency, a feature that worked great when survival meant finding food, not followers. But our brains haven't evolved as fast as our technology has—they're still stuck in a state of cognitive economy, which is to say the brain is still obsessed with saving mental energy. That's why we love life hacks and (supposed) five-minute habits. We're addicted to the illusion of progress because our brains release dopamine when we just *plan* to improve. That's right: buying the planner feels like working out. The brain throws a little party every time you think about *getting* better, not actually *doing* better.

All of which is why so many of us live in what I call the Productivity Theater. We're each of us starring in our own biopic titled *Coming Soon: My Potential.* We're going to revisit this topic of potential, but first, let's take a hard look at the hard work paradox.

We worship hard work...as long as someone else is doing it. We binge documentaries about Michael Jordan's 4 a.m. workouts while couch-eating popcorn at 11 p.m. We post quotes like "Trust the process" while actively ghosting it. But psychology has a receipt for this hypocrisy, namely the effort paradox: the more effort something requires, the more value we assign to it *after the fact.* We find meaning *after* the suffering, not before. The irony of this paradox is that if we reframed effort as *identity training*, not punishment, we'd start craving it, because effort is the only thing that lets us transform our self-image from "I hope I can" to "I always do."

The Neuroscience of Struggle

One of my favorite studies out of Stanford tracked students during problem-solving tasks.

The ones who *struggled longer before solving* the tasks didn't just remember the answers, they built deeper neural pathways for persistence. That's because struggle rewires us for strength. Every time we push through the hard part, our brain's anterior cingulate cortex (a.k.a. the struggle sensor) fires up. It's the same system that trains us to stay calm under chaos. So yes, every time you keep going when you want to quit, your brain literally updates your software. Effort is a neurochemical investment plan.

Which brings us to the lie of the hack. Don't get me wrong—I love hacks. But hacks without habits are like microwaving a steak and calling it a petit filet mignon. We live in an era when people spend more time optimizing their Notion templates than actually doing the to-dos listed inside of them. To be blunt, we've replaced discipline with aesthetics. And that has led us to a status quo where we've color-coded our success dashboard, but still, our goals are unaccomplished. That's the curse of illusory progress, that small dopamine spike we get from planning that tricks our brains into *feeling* accomplished.

Remember: a to-do list doesn't build confidence, *doing the things on it does*. The real hack?

Fall in love with boredom. Boredom is the tollbooth between "I started" and "I'm good at this."

Someone who exemplified this concept was Alex, the intern who outworked the algorithm. He was the first one into the office and the last one out, fueled entirely by energy drinks and mild existential dread. While others were optimizing their work–life balance spreadsheets, Alex was optimizing himself. He wasn't flashy, but he was curious. He didn't network up, he networked *around*. He learned everyone's job, not because he was told to, but because he couldn't stand not knowing.

One day, when his manager asked the team to brainstorm campaign ideas, Alex quietly stayed behind after the meeting and asked, "Can I take a shot at it tonight?" The next morning, he slid a mockup onto his boss' desk. It was a rough but brilliant draft. Two months later, it became the company's top-performing campaign of the year. When Alex finally got hired, the boss didn't say "You're creative" or "You're smart." He said, "You outworked the algorithm."

That line should be tattooed on every entrepreneur's forearm. Because even though we live in a world where AI can write a caption, summarize a meeting, and even generate a business plan, it can't care. It can't take initiative out of curiosity—it has to be instructed to do so. It can't inspire its coworkers. But *people* can inspire people thanks to a phenomenon called effort contagion. When people witness genuine effort, that inspires recip-rocal effort. In short, hard work spreads faster than apathy. (Thankfully!) This truth is why teams built on "grit energy" perform better over the long term than teams built on "flash energy." *That's* the quiet revolution no one's talking about. Effort is the last unfair advantage we have left.

Sarah found out the value of effort rather abruptly, when her startup took off—with growth came chaos, and suddenly, she was in back-to-back investor calls, trying to "scale culture" through dashboards and slogans. One day, after yet another meeting about KPIs and retention rates, she realized something chilling: she was leading, but she wasn't living. Her mentor, a retired Navy commander turned executive whis-perer, asked her, "When's the last time you actually touched the work?"

That question haunted her. So, the next morning, she ditched her calendar and went undercover—no title, no status. She spent a week shadowing her own team, answering support tickets, packing boxes, and joining product QA calls.

By the end of that week, her team had stopped seeing a CEO and started seeing a teammate. And *she* stopped seeing employees and started seeing impact. That week reactivated her intrinsic motivation circuit, the psychological engine that powers meaning through autonomy, mastery, and purpose. (Thank you, Daniel Pink, for introducing us to that concept. He's the author of *Drive: The Surprising Truth About What Motivates Us*.)

Despite what Sarah's experience proved, though, leaders often forget about the value of effort. You don't motivate through metrics, you moti-vate through *mirror neurons*—when people see you do the hard stuff, their brains light up in sync with yours. It's neuroscience's version of follow-the-leader. So, if you're a leader yourself, the next time your culture feels disconnected, don't buy another team-building platform, roll up your sleeves! And remember that while connection is contagious, so is complacency.

The Invisible Skill: Discomfort Tolerance

Every high performer secretly has a superpower. It's not talent and it's not IQ—it's discomfort tolerance. It's the ability to stay calm in the gap between "This isn't working" and "This worked."

A 2021 study in *Psychological Science* found that people who voluntarily exposed themselves to difficult experiences—from cold showers to public speaking—reported higher levels of self-efficacy and resilience than those who avoided discomfort altogether. Why? Because the brain doesn't grow in comfort, it grows in contrast. Every time you face discomfort and survive, your nervous system recalibrates: the fear signal gets quieter and the courage signal gets louder. You're literally reprogramming your perception of pain.

Think about it: if you can stay centered while sweating, failing, or being ignored, you're basically hacking your own nervous system. And in a world where everyone's addicted to dopamine hits, calmness under chaos is the new flex. So is hard work, even though hard work is hilarious. You spend eight hours polishing a PowerPoint that your boss then forgets to present. You post ten videos that flop and one that goes viral for the dumbest reason possible, like sneezing mid-sentence.

When that happens, humor is what keeps the grind from breaking you. Humor functions as cognitive reframing, giving you the ability to shift how you interpret stress. Laughter converts a threat into a challenge, chaos into a story, and struggles into a punchline. Every time you laugh mid-struggle, your brain releases serotonin and oxytocin, your built-in resilience boosters. Humor is hope with exquisite timing.

So yes, laugh while you're struggling! You're literally rewiring your brain for strength. The people who can find humor inside hardship don't just survive, they lead. And while you're letting yourself laugh, don't forget to show up. While "showing up" sounds painfully basic—the self-help equivalent of "drink water"—the psychology behind it is wild.

Every time you show up, even when you don't feel like it (maybe even *especially* when you don't feel like it), your brain releases a micro-dose of dopamine afterward. That's called behavioral activation. In other words, you don't *wait* for motivation, you *create* it by moving first. Unfortunately, though, most people have the order backwards. They say, "Once I feel motivated, I'll start." But neuroscience says, "Once you start, you'll feel motivated." It's like a biological prank the brain plays to separate the serious from the wishful.

When you show up repeatedly—even if imperfectly—your brain rewires around identity consistency. You stop asking yourself "Am I disciplined?" and start saying "I'm someone who doesn't skip." That's the subtle shift from action to identity. It's the loop that elite performers live in, because showing up isn't about intensity, it's about *integrity*. It's keeping a promise no one else even heard you make.

The Paradox of Effortless Confidence

Even though effortless confidence looks like a superpower, it's actually a side effect of showing up through every awkward, sweaty, unrewarded stage that came before. The inherent paradox is that the harder you work, the more natural you look. It's the illusion of effortless mastery, a psychological phenomenon where skill looks instinctive because repetition has automated it. When Kobe shot 1,000 free throws a day, it wasn't for the crowd, it was for his nervous system.

What people call "confidence" is actually muscle memory for self-belief. Continually keeping promises to yourself builds self-efficacy, the psychological currency of trust in your own ability. Every time you push through self-doubt, you deposit into that account. Eventually, the balance compounds so high that when life overdrafts you, you're still in the green. So actually, you're not "faking it till you make it." You're practicing it until it sticks. You're *making* it stick.

You can lose money. You can lose time. You can lose followers faster than your last viral post grew them. But you never lose what you built through effort. That's sweat equity, the invisible value of experience. Every failed project taught you something about resilience. Every rejection taught you something about framing. Every "almost" moment stretched your capacity for the real one.

When your brain experiences unexpected effort that leads to success, it triggers the reward prediction error—it says, "Whoa, I didn't think that would work, but it did!" The ensuing spike of surprise dopamine cements learning deeper than any easy win ever could. That's why your toughest seasons produce the most confident versions of you—by the end of those seasons, you haven't just built outcomes, you've built *proof of survival.* So, yes, the grind is exhausting. But the receipts it leaves behind? Priceless.

The Myth of Balance

Everyone wants "work-life balance," but here's the Al Gore moment (a.k.a. the inconvenient truth): you can't balance what's never been equal.

Balance implies symmetry, like life is some tidy pie chart, but real growth is lopsided. Messy. Seasonal.

Psychology calls it goal substitution theory. In a nutshell, your brain can't chase two conflicting goals with equal energy, so that means the season you're building something big might not be the same season when you feel perfectly balanced. And that's okay. The trick isn't balance, it's *alignment.* If your energy, effort, and emotion are going toward something meaningful, *im*balance becomes purpose. So, stop chasing balance and start chasing belief in your direction. The chaos will feel different when you know what it's building toward, even if sometimes that means quitting something intentionally.

A few years ago, I did that—I quit a project I loved. Or at least, I thought I loved it until I quit. It had started as a passion, but then it turned into a prison of endless work, no joy, and no curiosity. So, I walked away. Mind you, I felt guilty, like I had failed myself in my pursuit of discipline, but then I realized that quitting isn't failure when it's conscious. It's a form of psychological pruning—it's trimming the branches that block new growth. Behavioral science has an official term for this: cognitive reallocation. It frees up mental bandwidth to redirect your focus where it can actually thrive. It stops you from getting even further away from your path.

I didn't quit ambition, I quit noise. And that single act multiplied my focus tenfold. Sometimes the hardest work is walking away from work that no longer works.

WITHIN REACH TOOLKIT
The Compound Habit Formula

Here's the formula that drives every transformation you've ever admired:

Small Action × Daily Repetition × Emotional Connection = Exponential Identity Shift

In other words, consistency compounds faster than confidence grows. Let's break it down:

- **Small Action:** Your brain resists big leaps but accepts micro-motions. Start so small that it's almost insulting.
- **Daily Repetition:** Frequency beats intensity. The brain learns through rhythm.
- **Emotional Connection:** Dopamine amplifies learning. Anchor your efforts to your emotions, because your "why" will beat your willpower every time.

When you run this formula for 30 days, you're not just changing habits, you're reprogramming identity. This is how you'll go from "I'm trying to be confident" to "I just am."

WITHIN REACH TOOLKIT
The Motivation Loop Map

There's a neuroscience-backed cycle behind sustainable motivation. I call it the motivation loop:

1. Action → 2. Micro-Reward → 3. Momentum → 4. Identity Reinforcement → Repeat.

Most people get stuck waiting at the top because they want the reward first. But your brain doesn't trust words, it trusts *evidence*. Once you take action, dopamine is released, momentum grows, and your self-image upgrades to match. You start to *feel* like the person who follows through. That's the secret behind "grind culture" that actually works: not overworking, but *over believing* in motion.

Every generation rediscovers this truth in their own language. Our grandparents called it grit; our parents called it discipline; we call it the algorithm. But the principle never changes: effort compounds. Every time you choose the long game, you're quietly separating yourself from the noise. Because those who chase shortcuts will always run out of shortcuts, and when they do, you'll still be standing. Not because you're lucky, but because you lasted.

That's the paradox of hard work: it doesn't just build what you want, it builds who you needed to become to handle it. So, when someone says, "Work smarter, not harder," smile and whisper, "I do both." Because hard work still works even when no one's watching. *Especially* when no one's watching.

WITHIN REACH TOOLKIT
The Grind Grid™ + Compound Habit System

This tool in your kit is meant to help you transform effort into identity and avoid burnout disguised as productivity.

Step 1: Map your current grind grid.

Draw a 2 x 2 matrix:

- X-Axis: Impact (low → high)
- Y-Axis: Effort (low → high)

Plot your week—and be brutally honest. Most people live in the "high-effort/low-impact intersection, a.k.a. the busy trap.

Step 2: Reallocate 20% of your energy.

Shift one chunk of your time toward Quadrant 3: Smart Sweat. That's where the compounding magic happens and you combine high-effort actions with high-impact actions (and results).

Step 3: Install the compound habit formula.

1. Pick one habit that scares you but scales you up.
2. Shrink it until it's too easy to skip.
3. Attach an emotion to the action (i.e., "This habit makes me someone who keeps promises").
4. Track streaks, not perfection.

Step 4: Run the motivation loop.

Each day, take action, then celebrate your tiny win, then feel the momentum build and reinforce your identity. Then repeat. You'll find that momentum compounds faster than motivation fades.

Step 5: Audit yourself monthly.

Ask:

- "Did my effort compound or just consume me?"
- "Did I work toward growth or just toward exhaustion?"

Bonus Reflection Prompt: Write this in your journal:

"Where in my life am I mistaking busyness for progress?" That's where your next breakthrough lives.

Key Takeaways

- Hard work is identity training disguised as effort.
- Dopamine rewards motion, not perfection.
- Boredom is the entrance to mastery, not the exit.
- Effort is the last unfair advantage left.
- You can't skip the work meant to build you...and *that's* your edge.

The Long Way Home

Here's the uncomfortable truth about shortcuts: even when they work, they don't work on *you*. They get you somewhere faster, sure, but you arrive underbuilt. You skipped the part where the version of you who could handle it was supposed to be born. Because the point of the path was never just to get you there—it was to get you ready.

God doesn't rush what He intends to last—He's not interested in convenience, He's interested in character. And sometimes the only way to build character is to take the path that feels wildly inefficient, emotionally expensive, and spiritually confusing. That's the "hard way." The one with the extra hills, the awkward detours, the "Are You sure this is the plan?" prayers. But it's also the way that chisels your patience, tempers your pride, and forges your faith into something steel-strong.

The shortcut gets you to the destination. The hard way turns you into the kind of person who belongs there. So, take a deep breath, because we're about to talk about that hard way and about struggle, although not about just struggling for struggle's sake. It's about choosing the *refining* path.

CHAPTER 3

The Hard Way, On Purpose

Most of us spend our whole lives avoiding the hard way. We build apps, habits, and entire belief systems to make things easier; we want faster Wi-Fi, shorter lines, and smarter cars. (All of which unfortunately makes us lazier people.) But what if the hard way wasn't a setback? What if it was the syllabus?

I didn't realize this until I looked back at every major turning point in my life and noticed a pattern: nothing meaningful ever happened when things were easy. Not once. It's safe to say that for all of us, no growth story ever starts with, "Everything went according to plan and I felt no discomfort whatsoever." Instead, every defining moment is dressed like an inconvenience. In my case, those were the rejections that rerouted me, the detours that delivered me, and the "This can't be right!" season that somehow became the best thing that ever happened to me.

The truth is, God does His best work in the tension between "I'm not ready" and "Do it anyway." He's not impressed by your shortcuts—that's when He's trying to strengthen your spirit. The hard way is the gym where faith gets its reps in.

The Mineral Ridge Effect™: How Humble Beginnings Train Your Brain

I grew up in a small rural countryside called Mineral Ridge, Ohio. Maybe you're sitting there thinking, Rural countryside? Who is this guy—a time traveler from 1955? I wish! Because if I had a DeLorean, I'd go straight back to the '50s, grab a sports almanac, and tell my grandpa to invest in Apple.

But back to the point (not the future). I call it a "rural countryside" because Mineral Ridge doesn't technically qualify as a town anymore. It used to be one, but then it got demoted. Imagine a place being so uneventful that the U.S. Census ghosts it for 140 years. I looked it up: the first time Mineral Ridge shows up in the census is 1990, with a population of 3,900. Fast-forward thirty years to 2020, and the population was 3,951. That's it. Fifty-one new humans. Not exactly the kind of growth curve that inspires motivational posters.

My parents, John and Carol, were salt-of-the-earth people. A mechanic and a banker. They worked hard, earned modest wages, and lived paycheck to paycheck. College wasn't a family tradition; beer was. In fact, if alcoholism were a competitive sport, our family reunions could've qualified for the Olympics.

Back then, in our world, success meant keeping things close. You grew up near your parents, you got a job similar to theirs, you bought a house within walking distance, and BOOM! You'd made it. My aunt lived four doors down from my grandma and worked at the same place Grandma did. My dad lived fifteen minutes away, and you'd have thought he had joined the witness protection program. "What if I want to see you??" my grandma would yell over the phone in Slovak—which, for the record, is 60% consonants and 40% emotional damage.

My dad's reply? "Okay, mom, I love you." Click. Boundaries: established.

So, when you consider the backdrop—the rural countryside, the comfort of sameness, the low ceiling of "success"—it's fair to ask: how the hell did I make it out?

Let me pause and make one thing clear: my parents were incredible. They loved me unconditionally, gave me every ounce of what they could, taught me the value and habit of hard work, and taught me the kind of humility and gratitude that doesn't expire. But here's the truth most of us discover later in life: love can nurture you, but environment shapes you. I wasn't raised around ambition, I was raised around survival, and there's a psychological difference between the two.

Humble beginnings don't just teach gratitude, they wire the brain for constraint. Neuroscience calls this environmental priming; it's a tendency for your surroundings to train your perceptions of what's possible. When you grow up in a small place, your brain learns to make big dreams fit into small rooms. You internalize invisible limits. You confuse "realistic" with "reachable." And you start to believe the ceiling above you is structural when really, it's psychological.

But there's a flip side, a hidden gift: people who grow up in constraint often develop the superpower of "grittiness." You learn to make something out of nothing and to improvise your way through opportunity deserts. That's adaptive resilience! It's the brain's way of saying, "I'll build the path if I can't find one." So, while my upbringing didn't cultivate greatness on paper, it did something arguably better: it made me resourceful.

That's what I call the Mineral Ridge Effect™. It's when your environment limits your exposure but maximizes your resilience. It's like life's version of resistance training: uncomfortable, repetitive, and invisible to outsiders...until the day you need it most.

I used to pray for God to make things easier. Now I pray, "Make me stronger." Because I've learned that ease is overrated—it gives you comfort, not confidence. And confidence, as we'll talk about later, is built through evidence, through a collection of tiny moments that whisper, "I didn't think I could do that, but I did."

Sure, the hard way hurts. It humbles. It tests your patience and pokes every insecurity you thought you'd already graduated from. But it also does something miraculous: it reveals who you are when the applause stops and only purpose remains. When you pursue the hard way *on purpose*, it isn't masochism, it's mastery. It's saying, "If growth is the cost, I'll pay it in full." It's where you meet the future version of yourself and realize that your future self was waiting for you to endure, not for a miracle to occur.

For me, that realization came in waves, in hundreds of quiet moments. Like noticing that my classmates who dreamed bigger sounded weirdly confident. Or realizing that some people didn't think money was a miracle. Or that not everyone measured success by the proximity of their parents' house. Each of those micro-realizations cracked open my worldview a little more. If you zoom out, that's what psychological growth looks like. It's not sudden. It's seismic, yes, but also slow.

THE HUMBLE BEGINNINGS TOOLKIT™

When you're trying to outgrow your origin story, use this toolkit. And remember that the hard way *isn't* about staying comfortable. Which is the whole point, because staying comfortable is another kind of poverty. It doesn't show up in bank accounts, but it does show up in potential.

1. Label the ceiling.

Write down what you think is *normal* or *expected* based on your upbringing, income, career path, and lifestyle. Then ask yourself, "Who told me that was the limit?" Most ceilings are inherited, not real.

2. Reframe your scarcity.

Scarcity isn't failure, it's training. Every "lack" you grew up with became a rep in resourcefulness, adaptability, and empathy. Those are entrepreneurial superpowers in disguise.

3. Identify your own "Mineral Ridge moments."

Look for times when your limitations forced creativity. *That's* where resilience was born. Revisit them. Realize they're not constraints, they're evidence.

4. Redefine success in your own language.

If "making it" sounds like your family's definition and not yours, rewrite it. The moment you define success for yourself, you've already broken the psychological cycle of smallness.

Humble beginnings don't hold you back, they build you up differently. And they just don't hand you the manual—you have to write that yourself, the hard way, on purpose.

The Psychology of Doing the Hard Thing

When I tell people I switched from business to engineering, they usually tilt their heads like a confused golden retriever trying to understand quantum physics. "Wait—you went into engineering?" Yep. Once again, the hard way, on purpose.

Now, to be fair, this wasn't some Hollywood "I found my calling" montage where inspirational music swelled as I sprinted across campus in the rain. It was more like, "Hey, spreadsheets are cool and all, but what if I learned how the world actually works...like, literally?"

At the time, I didn't realize it, but that decision said more about me than any GPA ever could. It was the first breadcrumb in a pattern that would follow me my entire career: I kept doing the harder thing before I understood why.

When I first declared myself a business major, it made sense. It was practical. Marketable. My parents were proud. My friends approved. My future looked like a neatly laminated five-year plan. Then, one day (probably a Tuesday), I wandered into an Intro to Engineering lecture I wasn't even enrolled in. Ten minutes into the class, my brain was both melting and sparking. The professor was talking about forces, energy, and systems, and 90% of it sounded very similar to my grandma yelling at my dad. But something in me lit up. That was the day I realized: I didn't just want to understand business. I wanted to understand how things worked, the "why" behind the "what."

So naturally, I did what any rational college student would do: something extremely irrational. I switched majors from something predictable to something that required a minor in sleep deprivation. That first semester felt like trying to drink from a fire hose, except the fire hose was on fire. I went from color-coded lecture notes to three-hour labs where your entire grade depended on whether a circuit board felt emotionally stable that day.

The math stopped being friendly somewhere around the word "differential." Meanwhile, while everyone else was transferring out of engineering to "find themselves," I was transferring in, apparently, to lose myself. ("You better lose yourself in the music / The moment, you own it, you better never let it go / You only get one shot, do not miss your chance to blow / This opportunity comes once in a lifetime..." Sorry, I can't help myself.)

I didn't quit. I did fail tests, though. I stared at equations that looked like IKEA instructions written by aliens. And every time I hit a wall, I told myself, "You picked this mountain, so climb it." That was the first real-life manifestation of the grit I'd built in Mineral Ridge. Not the motivational poster kind, but the kind you earn quietly at 2 a.m., fueled by coffee and fear.

At the time, though, I didn't call it grit—I called it "panic with purpose." But that's exactly what grit looks like when it's still growing, messy, and unpolished. I wasn't chasing a title or a perfect GPA. I was chasing understanding. That tiny decision to lean into the harder thing instead of avoiding it became the blueprint for how I approached everything later in life. When projects got tough, when teams fell apart, when leadership meant taking the hits first...that early pain cave taught me something priceless: discomfort isn't a red flag, it's a compass.

The same holds true for you—every time you voluntarily do something difficult, something that stretches you instead of sparing you, your brain releases a cocktail of neurochemicals: dopamine, norepinephrine, and a dash of cortisol. That mix is your brain's way of saying, "Congrats, you didn't die! Here's some motivation for next time." But the key word here is "voluntarily." When you *choose* the challenge, your prefrontal cortex, your focus, and your decision-making center stay active. That's called cognitive reappraisal: you're reframing stress as a tool instead of a threat.

Over time, this rewiring becomes a psychological cheat code. Discomfort triggers attention, not anxiety. Enter the Dopamine Mastery Loop: Effort → Progress → Reward → Repeat. Grit isn't genetic, it's trained one do-it-the-hard-way decision at a time. It's character development, sure, but it's also *neural* development.

WITHIN REACH TOOLKIT
The Hard Way Filter™

Use this filter anytime you're deciding between the easy route and the one that scares you a little. If the answer is "Yes," proceed.

- Is this path going to stretch me more than it will protect me?
- Will I learn something even if I fail?

- Am I choosing curiosity over comfort?
- Will this make future me proud even if present me is tired?

The hard way, on purpose means choosing growth over comfort, curiosity over certainty, and effort over ego. You don't have to switch majors to learn that lesson—you just have to start paying attention to the moments when your instinct says "This might be too hard…" and then you have to do it anyway. Because often the smartest move is in fact *not* the easiest one—it's the one that teaches you who you are before you even realize it.

The Furnace and the Blueprint

The hard way has a funny way of revealing things that the easy way never could. You start out praying for relief and end up discovering *resilience.* You beg God to change the circumstance and He changes *you* instead. That's the secret nobody puts on the vision board: the struggle was never random, it was custom-fit. The long nights, the rejection emails, the "God, seriously?" seasons—they weren't just detours, they were design specs.

Once you've walked the hard road long enough, you realize it wasn't just building endurance, it was building evidence. Evidence that you can do hard things. Evidence that your faith works under pressure. Evidence that your wiring was never faulty, it was forged.

See, pain doesn't just toughen you, it *tunes* you. It rewires your instincts, calibrates your empathy, and redefines what "enough" even means. You start to see that every hardship was secretly a data point in God's experiment called *you.* You weren't mass-produced, you were hand-coded! And the same fire that refined you is proof that you're built different.

CHAPTER 4

Built Different: The Science of What Makes You, <u>You</u>

I used to think "built different" was just what people said when they couldn't dunk. Like, "Nah, bro, I'm built for dunking donuts, not basketballs." But the more I watched people (and by people, I mean me) spiral through life's PowerPoint presentations, the more I realized that "built different" isn't a flex, it's a survival strategy, and it's one that begins with seeing patterns rather than focusing on perfection. The stubbornness that kept me stuck? It was perseverance in disguise. The sensitivity that made me feel weak? Empathy with broadband. The overthinking that drove me crazy? That was strategy running diagnostics.

Let me paint the scene. It was a Tuesday, because of course it was. (I've realized Tuesdays are just Mondays that got held back a grade.) I was in a glass-walled conference room giving a presentation to my manager's manager's manager; basically, I was surrounded by the Avengers of middle management. The kind of people whose LinkedIn bios include phrases like "transformational leader" and "synergistic optimization," which usually means they own a standing desk and know how to talk unmuted on Teams.

I had rehearsed for days. I had mirror-smiled, timed my slides, even sprinkled in a joke designed to say, "I'm confident" while secretly whispering "Please validate me." *Click.* Next slide. *Click.* Next insight. Then, *BOOM...*

Black screen. Frozen deck. Brain buffering. Inside my head, my neurons started doing CrossFit. My inner critic was yelling, "This is why we shouldn't have majored in engineering!" My anxiety was opening tabs faster than Google Chrome. My confidence flatlined.

And then, somehow, I cracked a joke. Not rehearsed, not perfect—just human. The room laughed. The tension snapped. My confidence revived. And in that moment, I realized something wild: that unplanned stumble was more *me* than anything I'd prepared. And that's what being "built different" is. It isn't about being flawless, it's about how each of one of us responds when the deck freezes and the plan combusts.

There's no such thing as a "normal" blueprint even though from kindergarten onward, we were handed the same IKEA manual version of life:

Step 1: Get good grades.
Step 2: Go to college.
Step 3: Find a job that looks good on a mug.
Step 4: Pretend you're fine.

We were told there's a "normal" way to be a person. Like humanity came off one conveyor belt with the same parts, the same warranty, and one missing Allen wrench. But "normal" is a just convenient way of thinking, one that suits our evolutionary past. In psychology, it's the conformity bias, our brain's glitchy survival instinct that says, "Fit in or get eaten." Thousands of years ago, that logic made sense. If you were the cave dweller who decided to "do your own thing," you probably got eaten first. Today? You just get fewer likes.

But still, we spend years sanding down our edges to fit into boxes we were never designed for. We whisper things like "Why can't I focus like normal people?" and "Maybe I'm not cut out for this" and "If I just tried harder, I'd be more like them." Except that we aren't *supposed* to be just like everybody else. Each one of us was engineered with custom wiring, a.k.a. neurodiversity. I call it being a limited-edition model with unadvertised features. And in fact, the world loves to celebrate uniqueness—*until* it makes people uncomfortable. When that discomfort kicks in, then you might hear feedback disguised as "areas for improvement." Things like "Could you be a little less intense?" or "Maybe tone down the enthusiasm" or "Try to say less words in front of people." What all of those really mean, though, is "We'd prefer you in grayscale."

But psychology reminds us that authenticity—actually *being yourself*—is linked to lower stress, higher creativity, and stronger social bonds.

So, the next time someone says you're "too much," remember that "too much" is often just *a preview of innovation.*

Why Your Brain Is Basically a Messy Group Chat and Other Neuroscience Oddities

Picture your brain like a chaotic group chat that never sleeps. There's no admin and no mute button and everyone types all at once. In one corner, you've got The Risk-Taker, sending all-caps messages like, "LET'S QUIT OUR JOB AND START A CANDLE COMPANY!" Across the chat is The Cautious One, clutching spreadsheets and replying, "Bro, rent is due." Then The Overthinker shows up: "What if the candle explodes, our insurance lapses, and the mayor bans fire?" Meanwhile, The Therapist Voice softly chimes in: "What are we *really* avoiding here?"

It's chaos, but it's your chaos. The magic isn't in muting the noise; it's in knowing *who* to listen to *when.* That's called executive function, and it's the psychological equivalent of being your own CEO. When you forget something important, it's not because you're dumb, it's because your brain hit working memory overload. (And thanks to dopamine, you can recite all the lyrics to "Lose Yourself" but simultaneously forget your new coworker's name. One triggered the dopamine reward loop; the other didn't.)

Let's get nerdy for a second and define what parts of the brain do what:

- **Prefrontal cortex** → Your project manager. Plans, predicts, and vetoes the bad ideas before they escape from your mouth.
- **Amygdala** → The drama queen. Detects emotional smoke alarms before there's actual fire. Sometimes yells, "EVERY-THING'S ON FIRE!" when it's just a burnt Pop-Tart.
- **Hippocampus** → The historian. Keeps a museum of every embarrassing moment since first grade and is conveniently open 24/7.

Depending on your sleep, caffeine level, and proximity to your ex's Instagram story, these brain regions either work *together* or host a civil war. All of which means that you're not "scatterbrained," you're a biological startup running twelve open tabs overseen by one overloaded intern named Cortisol.

Psychologists call this internal orchestra self-complexity theory. It's the idea that we aren't one fixed personality, but rather a flexible collage of selves: the Work Self, the Chill Self, the "It's Sunday but my boss just texted me" Self. The more developed and integrated these selves are, the better we adapt to stress. But when we suppress them? We glitch.

Ever wonder why you feel weirdly empty after pretending to be composed all day? That's ego depletion, i.e., your mental battery draining from self-regulation overuse. So, the next time your inner committee starts arguing, don't panic! Just remember that chaos is the cost of consciousness. And remember that learning to moderate the group chat, *not* silence it, is emotional intelligence in action. (If all else fails, just have your committee answer this question: "If you had one shot or one opportunity / To seize everything you ever wanted in one moment / Would you capture it or just let it slip?")

Pain into Growth

Every superhero movie has that *one* defining moment—the radioactive spider, the lightning bolt, the tragic backstory. In real life, we just call that trauma. But here's the psychology twist: the very moments you thought broke you are often the moments that built you. That's because when something painful happens, your brain doesn't just "get over it," it *rebuilds itself* around it. This fortunate ability is neuroplasticity. It's your brain's way of saying, "Plot twist! Let's make it growth." Every time you faced chaos and didn't collapse, your brain literally rewired itself: it upgraded your defense systems, recalibrated your emotional responses, and logged a new data point as "We can survive that." That's why resilience isn't built in yoga studios or training conferences. It's built in the quiet moments when no one's clapping.

Research from trauma psychology backs this up: it shows that 70% of people who face major adversity experience something called post-traumatic growth. They have an increased appreciation for life, stronger relationships, and a redefined sense of purpose. In other words, what doesn't kill us does indeed make us stronger, *and* it makes us more self-aware, more empathetic, and more precise about what matters.

In other words, your pain becomes your blueprint. In much the same way, you can turn self-criticism into self-wins. For example, say you're like Andre—he's an email re-reader and a triple-checker. To the outside world, he's anxious overthinker. To neuroscience, he's a master of error detection circuitry. His brain lights up faster in the anterior cingulate cortex, the region responsible for noticing mistakes before they happen. That's not a flaw, that's a superpower. So, the next time someone tells you you're "too sensitive," "too analytical," or "too much," give your traits a job instead of a judgment.

The Science of Being Built Different

There's chemistry behind your quirks, from genetics (nature) to environment (nurture). All of us are born with a brain chemistry starter pack. Maybe you got extra dopamine receptors (hello, thrill-seeker!), or maybe you downloaded the anxiety expansion pack (yep—me, too). But genes don't decide your fate, they just draw the map. Per the heritability range theory, while you can't change the cards you're dealt, you absolutely *can* decide how to play them.

Of course, nature doesn't exist in a vacuum—this is where nurture comes in. Your wiring evolved in response to everything from your mom's tone of voice to that first heartbreak that turned you into a temporary philosopher. Every experience adjusted your emotional quotient sliders: confidence, trust, fear, ambition. But again, those sliders aren't locked in place. Your environment may have built your reflexes, but your reflection rebuilds your responses. That's why therapy, coaching, and journaling work. You're literally reprogramming your default settings.

Every time you choose discomfort over autopilot, your brain lays new wiring. That motivational quote you roll your eyes at—"Growth happens outside your comfort zone"—is actually a cornerstone of neuroscience. Your synaptic plasticity thickens when you attempt something new. Translation: courage rewires your brain. So, the next time you feel that friction of fear, remember, it's not resistance, it's rewiring in progress.

If you were to meet your eighteen year-old self today, that self wouldn't even recognize your current thought patterns! Because experiences don't just change what you believe, they change *how* you process reality. You're not a static personality, you're a living software update. And every version of you has been debugging the last one.

How to Figure Out What Makes You *You*

Most of us go searching for our "purpose" like it's hidden behind a pay-wall. We ask ourselves "What am I good at?" when the better question is "When do I feel most alive?" Because talent is mechanical, while energy is magnetic. Your *aliveness* is your compass. It's biology pointing you home.

The self-concordance theory is the idea that motivation lasts longest when your goals align with your true self, not your *should* self. Your *should* self says, "Be realistic!" Your *true* self whispers, "Be electric!" When your goals feel draining, it's not because you're lazy, it's because your nervous system can feel the misalignment. The body always knows it before the brain admits it.

So, if you're trying to figure out your purpose, forget those corporate self-assessment forms! Try answering these questions instead:

- When do I feel most alive, not just productive?
  → **Energy, not effort, reveals alignment.**

- What do people come to me for when they're stuck?
  → **That's social proof of your superpower.**

- What drains me faster than a bad Wi-Fi signal?
  → **The inverse of your gift is your kryptonite.**

- What do I automatically do that others struggle with?
  → **Your "easy" is someone else's Everest.**

- What problem am I obsessed with solving, even if I'm not being paid to solve it?
  → **Passion = curiosity that survived rejection.**

You don't *find* yourself, you *remember* yourself. Your wiring was always there; you just got good at muting it to make other people comfortable.

Now, decoding ourselves isn't simple, obviously. On top of that, most people hate vague advice. So, let's focus on the details. Specifically, on your DNA:

D = Distinct wiring
N = Natural energy
A = Adaptive resilience

What makes you weird is what makes you win! List three traits that once got you in trouble and then reframe them. (This is the D part of your DNA.)

OLD LABEL	REFRAMED AS A STRENGTH
"Impulsive"	"Acts decisively under pressure."
"Overthinker"	"Predicts outcomes before they happen."
"Sensitive"	"Processes emotional data others miss."

Bonus Round

"Distracted"   "Curiosity engine always scanning for opportunity."

"Stubborn"   "Unshakable conviction under uncertainty."

Reframing doesn't mean denial, it means data. You're changing your inner narrative from *problem* to *pattern.*

Now notice where time disappears. That's neural flow, when dopamine and norepinephrine team up to create focus that feels like fun. Write down three moments this week when you lost track of time. (This is the N part of your DNA.) What were you doing? Who were you with? That's chemistry syncing with purpose. This is your biological alignment report.

Resilience isn't bouncing back but rather bending without snapping. Your nervous system isn't weak for feeling stressed; it's adaptive for still *showing up.* List three moments you thought would break you but didn't. (This is the A part of your DNA.) Now list what each moment secretly taught you: pattern recognition, humility, patience, grit. That's your resilience dataset, a.k.a. the receipts for your strength.

When your D+N+A align, you've officially cracked your built different blueprint. But beware! It's all too common to misdiagnose your wiring, because we love to label ourselves like we're the clearance rack at TJ Maxx:

- "I'm lazy." – You just haven't found a goal that excites your dopamine circuit.
- "I'm too emotional." – You have high mirror-neuron sensitivity. That's empathy with broadband.

- "I can't focus." – You crave meaning, not monotony. That's nonlinear intelligence.
- "I'm inconsistent." – You're variety-oriented, the curiosity archetype of cognitive diversity.

Flipping the script is reframing your cognition: when you rename a trait accurately, you gain control of it. The story changes the state; the labels you accept become the limits you live.

Real-Life Archetypes

Although no two humans are wired the same, patterns do repeat. Let's meet the greatest hits of being built different:

The Quiet Observer

- Introverts don't command rooms, they decode them.
- Their superpower: reading micro-expressions in fewer than 200 milliseconds, which is faster than conscious awareness.
- Science calls it mirror-neuron attunement. I call it social Wi-Fi.

The Chaos Organizer

- Thrives when systems break.
- Feeds on adrenaline, caffeine, and unreasonable deadlines.
- When everyone else panics, they enter flow.
- Their nervous system treats crisis as clarity.

The Bridge Builder

- Turns strangers into teammates within five minutes.
- Empathy is their architecture.
- They measure success not in metrics but in connection density.
- They are living LinkedIn algorithms with a heart.

The Vision Translator

- Hears ideas no one else can hear and turns them into plans.
- Operates at the intersection of creativity × logic.
- Are often misunderstood until the world catches up.

The Soul Engineer

- Combines intuition and analysis.
- Can read energy and spreadsheets.
- Balances empathy with execution, a.k.a. leadership's secret weapon.

Each archetype is proof that "different" isn't defective, it's design. The goal isn't to be like everyone else, it's to operate like yourself, fully optimized. You can't unlock your uniqueness while you're cosplaying someone else's. The world doesn't need more duplicates!

Comparison is a sneaky thief, though, and it often interferes with our ability to surpass our archetype. Comparison dresses like motivation and steals our originality. You scroll through someone else's highlight reel, thinking, *They figured it out, so why can't I?* Meanwhile, they're scrolling through yours thinking the same thing. Psychologists call this social comparison theory. It's our primitive way of benchmarking self-worth through other people's success. It's how our ancestors survived in tribes. Now it's just how we ruin our Tuesdays.

When you start mimicking others, trying to act confident or fit the mold, your brain's default mode network (the imagination system that fuels originality) actually dims. You literally *think less creatively* when you copy. So, the next time you find yourself shrinking to fit, remember: the cost of imitation is innovation. Also keep in mind that being built different means you'll often feel out of sync. That's because you're *not* background noise, not at all—you're a different frequency entirely. Seeing as you're building something no one's built before, there's no comparison metric, so don't even try to play the comparison game.

WITHIN REACH TOOLKIT
Your Built Different Blueprint

Time to go from awareness to action! This is your personal operating system audit, your manual for being *you* on purpose:

1. Create your wiring map.

Draw three overlapping circles labeled Wiring, Energy, and Resilience. At the intersections, jot down examples:

- Wiring: Traits that once felt inconvenient but now fuel results.
- Energy: Environments, people, and topics that feel like caffeine for your soul.
- Resilience: Proof of survival, the stuff you overcame that would've made others tap out.

The overlap is your Built Different Zone. It's where biology meets purpose.

2. Run one weekly experiment.

Pick one trigger that usually spirals you: a tough conversation, a stressful deadline, or even just silence. Instead of reacting, observe it like a scientist and ask yourself, "What data is this giving me about how I'm built?"

Observation is greater than (and more effective than) judgment.

Observation is how you convert emotion into insight.

3. Build your operating manual.

Create your own The OS of Me profile:

SYSTEM FIELD	MY DATA
Best conditions	When I thrive and feel most alive.
Low-battery signs	What happens when I'm drained or disconnected.
Reset protocol	My quickest way to recharge (i.e., movement, silence, creativity, connection).
Superpower in action	The environments where I create disproportionate value.
Kryptonite	The patterns that drain me or dull my instincts.

This is cognitive optimization: by mapping these patterns, you'll reduce your decision fatigue, which is a measurable mental drain that costs up to 30% of your productivity daily. That's a huge savings!

4. Share it.

Tell one person what you've discovered about your wiring. This could be a friend, mentor, or coworker. Why is this sharing so important? According to research from Harvard's Human Connection Lab, authentic self-disclosure increases trust and likability by up to 32%. Vulnerability doesn't weaken credibility, it *deepens relatability.*

5. Recalibrate monthly.

Set a calendar reminder titled "Update Built Different OS." Review what worked, what drained you, and where your natural flow showed up most often. You'll notice patterns and new algorithms emerging from your own behavior. This is your personal evolution log.

Let's circle back to that frozen PowerPoint for a minute. When my slides died and my brain hit panic mode, I didn't respond like a professional, I responded like *me*: sarcastic, slightly unhinged, wired for humor under pressure. And it worked.

Afterward, my boss said, "You handled that like a pro." But I remember thinking, *No, I handled that like John.* The sarcasm, the nervous humor, the overpreparation—none of those were flaws to fix. Those quirks were evidence of wiring. Every time life had glitched on me, I'd been unknowingly collecting calibration data. Every failure that had screamed "You're not enough!" was actually my brain building tolerance for chaos. The moment when the PowerPoint froze didn't prove I was perfect—it proved I was programmable. And so are you.

CATEGORY	REFLECTIVE PROMPTS	NOTES/INSIGHTS
Wiring	What three traits have people labeled "too much" or "not enough"? How could they be hidden advantages?	Flip flaws into features. Reframe through function.
Energy	When do I feel "in flow"? What environments, people, or tasks amplify my focus?	Identify patterns that trigger dopamine + purpose.
Resilience	Which past setbacks taught me something I couldn't have learned otherwise?	Document recovery scripts, i.e., your personal bounce-back algorithms.
Application	Where can I apply my Built Different Blueprint (career, relationships, creativity)?	Translate self-awareness into decision strategies.
Growth zone	What's one discomfort I'll intentionally face this month?	Growth = repetition of discomfort + reflection.

Bonus Tool: The "Trait Translator"

Whenever you're tempted to self-criticize, run your thought through this formula:

Old Story: "I'm too ___."
New Translation: "My brain is wired for ___, which means I need ___ to thrive."

Examples:

"I'm too emotional." → "My brain is wired for empathy, which means I need boundaries to thrive." "I'm too intense." → "My brain is wired for deep focus, which means I need recovery periods to recharge."

Psychologically, this reframing triggers cognitive reappraisal, the most effective emotion-regulation strategy in neuroscience. It's not self-help fluff. It's self-hack *science*.

You don't need to become someone different—you just need to understand that you already are different. You're built different for a reason, not to outperform everyone else, but to build something no one else can. And the moment you stop apologizing for how you're wired, everything that once felt out of reach will start falling into place. Because what's within reach...was always you.

Blueprints Don't Build Themselves

Of course, self-awareness doesn't finish the job—it *starts* it. Knowing who you are is powerful, but until you put the various pieces together, awareness is just potential with a good personality. You can map your wiring, decode your DNA, and understand every psychological theory from Maslow to Marvel, but you still have to make an effort to build up your confidence. The way you do that is with repetition and motion. It's an unabashedly messy, awkward, faith-meets-friction process—in other words, the "assembly required" part of the Built Different Blueprint.

CHAPTER 5

Assembly Required: The Untold Truth About Confidence

Confidence is an ongoing construction project. You don't wake up one morning suddenly sure of yourself—you wake up, question everything, spill coffee on your shirt, and choose to show up anyway. *That's* confidence. Confidence is assembled one small act of courage at a time, usually while your inner critic is narrating the blooper reel. And God, with His very specific sense of humor, tends to hand out blueprints labeled "Trust Me" with no visible assembly instructions.

But that's by design. Confidence isn't about having all the pieces, it's about believing they'll fit together once you start—you don't build faith because you *feel* ready, you build it so you can *become* ready. Confidence is learned exposure therapy. It's the brain slowly realizing, "Oh, rejection doesn't actually kill us. It just feels like spicy embarrassment for a bit."

We treat confidence like it's something other people were issued at birth while we were out sick that day. But if you've ever met a toddler convinced they can fly, you know confidence isn't about ability. It's about delusion, optimism, and just enough naivety to think, *Yeah, I can probably do that.* And you know what? Probably you can. (Although no, you can't fly unassisted.)

Here's the cheat code: Confidence = Evidence × Exposure. The more proof you collect that you can handle hard, uncomfortable, or awkward situations and the more often you repeat handling those situations, the more your brain stops interpreting discomfort as danger. Of course, like any IKEA shelf, you will absolutely build up your confidence wrong the first time you try to do it. You'll misread the manual, snap a piece in half, maybe cry a little. But you'll also *learn*, and next time, your brain will remember where the tricky parts are. That's growth, not failure.

The False Advertising Department (a.k.a. Everyone's Faking It)

You know those people who walk into a room looking like they've never known doubt? They have perfect posture, balanced energy, and the kind of LinkedIn headshot lighting that just follows them around. But the reality is that half of them are bluffing and the other half are terrified you'll find out they're bluffing. And somehow both halves end up running the meeting.

Confidence, at least at first, is performance art. It's not pretending to be someone else, it's auditioning for the role of the person you're becoming. This is embodied cognition, the idea that your body can trick your brain. Stand tall long enough, and your nervous system goes, "Ah, yes, we must be capable of handling this" and your thoughts follow suit. That's why the ol' "fake it till you make it" works.

Contrary to popular interpretation, though, you're not faking competence, you're rehearsing courage. You're teaching your nervous system a new normal one deep breath, one awkward introduction, one trembling presentation at a time. Confidence is a feedback loop where action creates evidence and evidence changes belief. And then belief fuels action again.

Think of it like karaoke: the first verse sounds shaky and off-beat, but by the second chorus, you're suddenly Adele, or at least, you're confidently pretending to be. In that spirit, here's a tagline to post on your mirror: "Act like the person you're becoming. Your brain will eventually stop arguing and take notes."

If confidence *did* come with instructions, they'd be something like this:

Step 1: Identify the lie.

"I'm not ready."
"I'm not qualified."
"I'm too late."

Acknowledge the truth: you just don't have enough *evidence* yet. Your brain is running outdated software—it's referencing a version of you from five years ago who still flinched at public speaking or got nervous sending an email to leadership. Update your mental OS. You've survived way more since then!

Step 2: Tighten one screw.

Send the email. Ask the question. Post the cringe video. Momentum eventually leads to perfection! You don't need a 12-step plan, you need a single push that tells your brain, "We're doing this now."

Step 3: Expect missing parts.

You'll never feel 100% ready. If you wait until you do, your dreams will expire faster than your Amazon return window.

Step 4: Reread the manual.

Confidence swings. Some days, you'll feel like a walking TED Talk; other days, you'll feel like a phone that only has 3% of life left in it. That's fine. Recalibrate. Reflection keeps you aligned.

Step 5: Tighten as needed.

Confidence loosens over time. Retighten through courage reps: small, consistent acts that remind your brain who's driving.

Every time you take a micro-risk, raise your hand, say no, or apply before you're "ready," you're literally rewiring your neural pathways. That's synaptic pruning, the process of the brain cutting out old fear patterns and reinforcing new ones through repetition. Think of your fear responses like old Wi-Fi networks: you don't need to delete them, you just need to stop auto-connecting.

The Science of Confidence

Your brain's built-in alarm system, the amygdala, is basically a prehistoric drama queen. Its one job is to keep you alive, but unfortunately, it can't tell the difference between an actual threat and mild embarrassment. To your amygdala, public speaking = bear attack. So when your heart races before a presentation, just know your nervous system is loading a two-million-year-old survival program.

But here's the magic: every time you survive something uncomfortable, your brain performs neural adaptation, an upgrade that says, "We've met this bear before." That's why the third presentation feels easier than the first. Exposure therapy lets us deliberately repeat actions and thereby desensitizes the brain's alarm system. Confidence, then, is not about removing fear, it's about retraining your trigger sensitivity to fear. It's muscle memory for courage. You're not getting braver, you're just getting familiar with fear.

Neuroscience agrees with this: when you act in spite of fear, you're engaging your prefrontal cortex, the part of your brain that makes logical decisions. The more you activate it under stress, the more it learns to override the emotional panic center. Every awkward email, every shaky "I'll take it from here," every small step into discomfort is you running internal software updates. By the time your brain catches up, you're already halfway through doing the thing you thought you couldn't do.

Sometimes fear leads to over apologizing. That was once the case for Maya—she used to apologize when other people bumped into her. Her existential default setting was "Sorry!" Sorry for asking questions, sorry for existing too loudly, sorry for needing a minute to think. But she got tired of being in a constant state of "Sorry!", so she built a simple system she called the Evidence Log. Every time she did something even mildly brave—spoke up in a meeting, said no to a weekend favor, asked for feedback without getting a panic attack—she wrote it down. At first, her log looked ridiculous:

- "Didn't back out of lunch."
- "Said my idea out loud even though my voice shook."
- "Didn't say sorry when the barista got my order wrong."

But three months later, her notebook wasn't a diary of fear, it was a résumé of proof. She had pushed past her natural bias toward negative recall. We all have this—it's called the negativity bias, and it's the tendency to remember one insult more accurately than we can remember ten compliments. The only antidote is to do what Maya did: counterweight that bias with recorded wins.

And there's the classic overthinker, like Andre. He prepped for interviews like he was going to be testifying at a Senate hearing—he'd study company reports, memorize talking points, even rehearse spontaneous laughter. (Which is the least spontaneous thing you can rehearse, really.)

But his perfectionism had a side effect: paralysis. He never felt ready enough. So, I told him about the 70% Rule: if you feel 70% ready, that's *ready enough.* Your brain doesn't need perfection to act, it needs permission. Ten interviews later, Andre had come to embody confidence calibration—that 70% had become his new 100%. "Done awkwardly" is better than "planned perfectly."

Another one of my clients, Alexis, got promoted before she thought she was ready. During her first meeting as a manager, she froze. The team stared. The silence was louder than her imposter syndrome. Her brain screamed, "You're not supposed to be here!!" But instead of pretending, she said, "I don't have all the answers, but we'll figure it out together." And the room exhaled.

That single act of authentic vulnerability flipped Alexis from insecure to influential because vulnerability creates trust and trust creates momentum. That's called psychological safety, a concept developed by Harvard researcher Amy Edmondson. It's an environment where people feel safe taking risks. Confidence is contagious in those spaces. Alexis' team didn't follow her because she had all the answers, they followed her because she was brave enough to admit she didn't.

Other people tend to overcorrect when they're panicking internally. Take Jesse—he was a guy who overcompensated for his lack of confidence. Loud handshake, louder opinions, constant performance. But underneath, his self-worth was hanging on by a thread and a caffeine drip. When he finally burned out, he learned he'd been engaging in pseudo-confidence. That's the performance of certainty to avoid the discomfort of doubt. It looks like leadership but feels like exhaustion. Real confidence, in contrast, doesn't drain you—it grounds you.

So Jesse decided to reboot his approach. He started small: he paused before answering, asked questions instead of flexed facts, and traded arrogance for curiosity. Turns out, humility isn't the opposite of confidence, it's the upgrade.

The Confidence Trap

Myth: Confidence means never doubting yourself.
Reality: Confidence means acting even as doubt sits in the front row and heckles you.

Almost every high performer wrestles with imposter syndrome. Fun fact: it affects about 70% of people at some point, including CEOs, surgeons, and apparently every single person who's ever used Microsoft Excel in front of someone else. Imposter syndrome is just the brain's way of saying, "Congratulations! You're operating beyond your previous evidence level." But really, you're not broken, you're *expanding*.

Leadership Edition: Confidence Transfer

Confidence runs on a dopamine feedback loop: small win → dopamine spike → brain flags it as rewarding → you repeat the action. Each time you do, your identity is further cemented: "I'm the type of person who does hard things on purpose and survives." That's identity-based confidence. It's not a mood. It's a *reputation* you build with yourself, because you can't outsource confidence—borrowing other people's praise will only last until they stop clapping. True confidence comes from self-issued receipts. This kind of self-efficacy is the belief in your ability to execute behaviors necessary for specific outcomes. Think of confidence as emotional compound interest: the earlier you invest, the more you'll earn in the future.

Now let's say you're at the leadership level. At this point, confidence evolves from self-trust to trust projection. You've already built your personal version of the IKEA shelf—now your job is to teach others how to find their missing screws without losing their sanity. You can do that by self-regulating. Your nervous system is contagious, and during stressful moments, the brains of everybody on your team are scanning *you* for cues on how much danger they're in. That's co-regulation, a concept in emotional neuroscience that explains how humans sync heart rates, cortisol levels, and even micro-facial expressions in shared environments. If you're the calmest person in the room, you become the Wi-Fi for everyone else's nervous system.

When a crisis hits, leaders often think, *I have to know what to say.* But what your team really needs is to feel what you *believe.* Your composure is their permission to exhale. So, instead of saying "Don't panic," model steady breathing, ground your tone, and break problems into small, solvable steps. And remember that you're regulating an ecosystem of brains. Also remember that the most confident leaders are usually the

WITHIN REACH TOOLKIT
The IKEA Confidence Model™

STEP	PIECE	DESCRIPTION	PSYCHOLOGICAL HACK
1. Inventory check	What's missing—skill, experience, or courage?	You can't assemble what you haven't named.	Use metacognitive labeling—naming the emotion reduces its power. Example: "This is anxiety, not a sign that I'm unqualified."
2. Micro-wins first	Stack tiny victories.	Confidence compounds like interest.	Each micro-win triggers dopamine reinforcement, teaching your brain that progress = pleasure.
3. Align and tighten	Reevaluate your self-talk.	When you spiral, adjust your mindset, not your mission.	Try cognitive reappraisal—reframe "I'm nervous" into "I'm energized." Same biology, different story.
4. Show up messy	Progress loves mess. Perfection loves delay. Publish, then polish.	Imperfect action reprograms avoidance circuits faster than perfect planning does.	Use your reticular activating system to recognize that action is the goal.
5. Repeat the build	Confidence expires if not renewed.	Treat confidence like it's a gym: if you skip reps, you'll lose gains.	Repetition + reflection = neural consolidation.

ones humble enough to say, "I could be wrong, but here's where I'd start." That's not weakness, that's psychological transparency.

Unfortunately, even though confidence does *not* equate to certainty, social media has turned confidence into just that: a filtered, flexed, and #SelfLove performance art. But what we often call "confidence" online is really just carefully curated pseudo-certainty. Somewhere between the girl boss reels and the alpha male podcasts, we turned confidence into cosplay. We stopped asking "Do I believe in myself?" and started asking "Do I *look* like I believe in myself?" But confidence without humility becomes arrogance. And arrogance is just insecurity wearing designer cologne.

True confidence sounds quiet. It's the calm "I got this" whispered before a tough conversation. It's admitting aloud, "I don't know, but I'll find out." It's staying when everyone else leaves. This authentic confidence is grounded in clarity, not comparison. It's less "Watch me!" and more "Walk with me."

The Confidence Equation

Confidence = Action → Evidence → Identity

1. Action: Do the thing before you feel ready.
2. Evidence: You survive, learn, and file the proof.
3. Identity: "I'm the kind of person who can handle hard things."

That loop, repeated enough times, redefines your entire nervous system's story. Your amygdala eventually stops screaming "We're dying!" and instead says "We've been here. We're fine." But of course, confidence requires constant organization and constant reassembly, like the furniture you keep rebuilding every time life changes apartments. Some days, the screws don't fit. Some days, the manuals are in Swedish. Some days, you build it backward, stare at it, and start over.

And that's the point, because confidence is built through chaos. Every wobble, every do-over, every "Maybe I shouldn't have said that" moment is data. Your brain is cataloging survival stories. Eventually, you step back from your slightly uneven masterpiece and realize something beautiful: you didn't need to be born confident. You just needed to keep showing up with the tools you had. So, grab your metaphorical Allen wrench and tighten your courage screws!

WITHIN REACH TOOLKIT
Confidence Reassembled

ACTION STEP	PROMPT	WHY IT WORKS	YOUR NOTES
Inventory	What triggers my self-doubt most often?	Metacognition: Naming the source of fear activates your prefrontal cortex, lowering emotional reactivity.	
Micro-wins	What's one small action I can take today to prove I'm capable?	Dopamine reinforcement: Small wins create chemical proof that effort = reward.	
Reflection	What situation gave me evidence of progress recently?	Memory reconsolidation: Revisiting wins rewires how your brain stores confidence data.	
Tighten	What story am I telling myself that needs rewriting?	Cognitive reappraisal: Reframing self-talk changes emotional response patterns.	
Rebuild	What's the next challenge I'll use to stretch my comfort zone?	Neuroplasticity: Discomfort signals new growth pathways forming.	

Pro Tip: Your brain will always choose comfort over confidence. That's fine. Let it whine while you win.

Bonus: 5-Minute Confidence Reset (Use Before Any Big Moment)

1. **Breathe like a Navy SEAL:** 4 seconds in, 4 seconds hold, 4 seconds out, 4 seconds hold. This is "square breathing," and it resets your amygdala.
2. **Do a posture check:** Shoulders back, chin level. Body position cues mindset.
3. **Recall micro-evidence:** Say three sentences starting with "I've done harder things than _____ [whatever the task at hand is]."
4. **Visualize the outcome:** Per a Harvard study, 10 seconds of success imagery = 30% higher task performance.
5. **Smile, even if it's fake:** Your brain doesn't know the difference. That's facial feedback theory at work.

The Blueprint Was Just the Beginning

Confidence is proof that you've started building. But *potential* is proof that God's not finished yet. See, confidence gets you moving, but potential is what you're moving toward. It's the stretch between who you are and who you're still becoming, the divine "more" that's wired into every one of us. If confidence is constructed through repetition, potential is revealed through obedience. It's not about waiting for the perfect timing, funding, or opportunity, it's about stewarding what's already in your hands and trusting God to multiply it.

The world loves to talk about "untapped potential" like it's a nice compliment. But untapped potential isn't a compliment, it's a caution sign. It's the reminder that raw material doesn't change the world until you build something with it. You've learned how to assemble belief—now it's time to activate purpose. Because there's a message, one that found me when I least expected it, one that flipped how I see talent, faith, and what I—what we—call "enough." It's about *maximizing* your potential, i.e., turning what God placed within your reach into something the world can't ignore.

CHAPTER 6

The Message That Changed My Life

It's wild how one message can rewire your entire operating system. Not a TED Talk. Not a sermon with fog machines and key changes. Just a simple moment when God slides truth across the table and says, "You've got more in you—now do something with it." When this happened to me, up until then, I had been thinking that potential was a personality test result, something you *had.* But then I realized that potential isn't what you have, it's what you *honor.* It's the gap between your comfort zone and your calling and whether or not you're willing to bridge that gap.

Most of us pray for purpose while ignoring the projects that would grow it. We wait for a sign while Heaven's like, "Cool, but I gave you lungs, ideas, and Wi-Fi—maybe start there?" At some point, "I'll do that someday" needs to turn into "Today I start," and so this is the chapter where potential stops being hypothetical. Because it's less about being gifted and more about being *responsible* for the gift. Once you understand that, potential stops being pressure and starts becoming proof.

The Free Food Decision

I was nineteen and two semesters deep at the University of Toledo when I met Mike, my new resident advisor. And one day (definitely a Tuesday), he pulled me aside and asked me if I had ever thought about being a resident advisor myself. I didn't know what he meant by that, not really, but when he said, "Free room and board," I said, "I'm in" faster than a broke college kid can microwave ramen. I didn't ask about duties, rules, or training. Honestly, he could've slipped in "minor military commitment" and I still would've saluted if it came with unlimited meal swipes.

A few weeks later I found out what the fine print was: training. (Which, for college students, is just a polite way of saying "You can't leave.") During one of those sessions, a guest speaker walked in. No slides, no smoke machine, just presence. Calm voice. Steady eyes. And a message that somehow sliced through the fog of Mountain Dew and dorm noise in my nineteen-year-old brain. Her message was simple. *Painfully* simple. Three words, but they hit like a lightning bolt to my self-doubt: You. Have. Potential.

That was it. Just three words and a punctuation rhythm that landed harder than any pep talk I'd ever heard. If you're thinking, *That's it?*, yeah, same. It wasn't exactly Oprah's "You get a car!" moment. But for me, it was the first time anyone had handed me the cheat code to self-worth. For the first time, I thought, *Wait... Maybe I* can *be more than what my parents were. Maybe I* can *outgrow the zip code I came from.* And those tiny, seemingly ordinary words "You. Have. Potential." became the spark that started everything. Funny how the smallest sentence can wake up the loudest part of your life.

At the end of the speaker's talk, she gave everyone a small blue pin that said those exact words. I pinned mine to my backpack like it was an Olympic medal for emotional growth. I wish I could tell you I still have that pin, but that would be a lie and my nose doesn't need more reasons to grow. What I *do* still have is the message. Because without that moment, there's a real chance you wouldn't be reading this book right now. (Mystery Woman, if by some cosmic Wi-Fi glitch you're reading this, please reach out. You changed everything.)

And now I'd like to upgrade what she said and add to it a bit: You. Can. *Maximize.* Your. Potential. Having potential is fantastic. Maximizing it is elite. Because potential is like an unused gym membership: full of promise but useless without sweat.

The Pursuit of Potential

Legendary UCLA coach John Wooden once said, "Don't measure yourself by what you have accomplished, but by what you should have accomplished with your ability." That quote wrecked me (in the best way). It means success is about squeezing every drop out of what you've been given. You can't outsource that. You can't compare that. Because who cares if you "beat" everyone else if you only used 70% of *you*?

Nobody embodied this concept more than Tiger Woods. In 1997, he won the Masters by a record-breaking twelve strokes. (For non-golfers, that's like winning a marathon, showering, grabbing brunch, *and* still finishing before the second-place winner even crosses the line.) After his historic win, a reporter asked, "So Tiger, what's next?" And Tiger—calm, serious, borderline robotic—said, "I'm going to fix my swing."

The reporter blinked. "Wait...what? You just destroyed everyone. Why change anything?" Tiger: "Because I'm not the best I can be."

Mic. *Drop.* That's when the world realized Tiger wasn't chasing trophies. He was chasing potential. And for the next fifteen years, he *was* the best in the world. (Then, later, he chased a few other things, but that's another story for another book.)

But when it comes to potential, there's a twist! Your brain loves potential as long as you never use it. Why? Because using it introduces the risk of failure and failure feels like *danger.* So instead, your brain gives you a decoy win. It convinces you that thinking about doing something is the same as doing it. It's an illusion of progress. When you're planning, prepping, or color-coding your notion board, your brain releases the same dopamine hit as you'd get from actually finishing something. It's biology's way of handing out participation trophies.

That's why Tiger was rare—he wasn't addicted to the feeling of progress, he was addicted to the *pursuit* of it. The discomfort of not yet being his best was the motivator. But most of us aren't quite there, at least not yet. We're still in the ego protection phase, the one where it's easier to start projects than finish them. That's often perceived as laziness, but really, our brains would rather protect our potential than test it. Except growth only ever comes from maximizing potential, and we're not going to get there by forever just protecting it.

WITHIN REACH TOOLKIT
Maximize Your Potential

Use this quick self-audit to see where your potential's hiding and how to pull it out of hibernation:

1. Audit your output.

Ask yourself, "What percentage of my effort am I actually giving?" Be ruthless. Most people *think* they're at 90% when really, they're closer to 60%.

2. Spot the comfort traps.

Where have you traded competence for comfort? The moment you said "I'm good at this," you probably stopped growing at it.

3. Set "swing fix" goals.

Like Tiger, pick one skill you've already mastered and make it 10% better. Not 100%. 10%. Small, consistent tweaks compound fast.

4. Measure by ability, not approval.

Don't grade yourself against other people's highlight reels. Measure yourself against what you're truly capable of.

5. Replace "have" with "maximize."

Write this somewhere visible: "I don't just have potential, I maximize it." Bonus points if you print it on a pin.

Potential isn't a compliment, it's a contract. One that says: "You've been given something—now *do* something with it." Rather than another motivational quote, you just need to keep your promise to your potential. Because when you do and when you maximize it for all it's worth, you put yourself in positions where you may get a question from a stranger that sets your life on a path you never even thought was possible.

When Potential Starts Speaking First

The funny thing about potential is that once you start honoring it, it starts talking for you. You walk into rooms differently. You stop auditioning for belonging and start operating from it. Essentially, when you finally believe you're built for more, your energy shifts before your words do. People can feel when you've stopped shrinking to fit; they can sense when you've made peace with your calling.

That's what potential does when it's activated: it leaks. It shows up in your posture, your tone, your patience, your prayer life. It's spiritual physics—the inner world starts rearranging the outer one. The world hears you *arrive*. Presence is projection, not performance. It's the invisible signal your spirit sends out before your voice even catches up. When potential becomes presence, your purpose finally starts speaking for itself.

CHAPTER 7

The Room Knows Before You Speak

Every room has a language, and it starts speaking before you do. You can feel it when you walk in: the hum, the glance, the quick internal scan that every human performs in zero point two seconds to decide, "Safe or threat? Leader or background noise?" Basically, before your words ever hit the air, your energy has already given a TED Talk—your posture, your eye contact, your peace (or your panic) make the point louder than any intro slide ever could. That's emotional contagion, the science of how your internal state leaks into the atmosphere. It's also what Scripture calls *fruit.*

Presence is about vibration. It's the silent testimony that says, "I know who sent me here." That kind of confidence can't be faked because it's forged in the quiet chapters we've already walked through: the grind, the faith, the furnace, the blueprint. The room doesn't respond to your résumé, it responds to your resonance. And when who you *are* finally aligns with why you're there, everyone recognizes that. Everyone recognizes *you.*

We like to think communication starts with words, but it doesn't— communication starts with our nervous system group chats. Humans are basically emotional Wi-Fi routers: we broadcast energy all day long and everyone else's nervous system auto-connects, no password required. You've met the types:

- The person who radiates calm authority. Their presence feels like a noise-canceling headphone for your anxiety.
- The person who radiates frantic urgency. Their presence feels like 12 browser tabs open on your soul.
- And then there's always that one coworker radiating "Four iced coffees and one existential crisis!"

I'll use a vignette from my own life to illustrate how effectively our unintentional energy broadcasting works. I once walked into a boardroom with a big client. The stakes were high and the room was full of people who smelled like quarterly bonuses and generational wealth. I was ready. Deck polished. Shoes shined. My jokes were strategically placed at four-minute intervals for maximum likability ROI. And my confidence level was a ten out of ten.

But then my internal Wi-Fi crashed. It was like my nervous system whispered, "Oh, you thought we were ready? That's cute." My breathing sped up. My heart started buffering. My laugh came out three octaves too high.

And the room felt it. Before I even said, "Good morning," they subconsciously registered my signal: uncertainty. The entire scene was a textbook illustration of the fact that our energy always leaks first. Words are a delayed transmission of how we feel—our nervous system has already introduced itself before our mouth gets the chance.

That meeting didn't flop because my ideas were bad, they flopped because my *frequency* was off. My signal said, "I'm not sure I belong here," and the room politely agreed. I left that day with one painful but permanent lesson: confidence isn't something you announce, it's something you regulate.

All of this is so ironic, because although we spend our entire lives learning how to talk, no one ever teaches us how to transmit. If we *could* transmit effectively, we could find ourselves on a rocket fueled by favor and grace chasing our dreams through the stars.

Presence Isn't Personality, It's Physics

We've confused presence with personality like it's some charisma gene we either inherit or don't. We think presence is about being extroverted, loud, or one of those people who somehow manages to look photogenic in their driver's license picture. But presence is *physics*, not personality. It's the invisible alignment between our internal world and our external expression the moment when our energy and our message match.

If confidence was the IKEA furniture we built in the last chapter, presence is the gravitational field holding it all together—that unspoken pull that makes people lean in instead of checking their phones. When your presence and energy are congruent, people trust you even if you mess up words, drop your notes, or accidentally say "orgasm" instead of "organism" in your biology presentation. (True story-tenth-grade John never recovered.) In contrast, when your energy and your words *don't* match, your nervous system sends out static. And people feel it.

Your nervous system is basically your emotional Wi-Fi router. Presence happens when your router, your device, and your content are all synced. The nervous system simply cannot fake alignment! It's either broadcasting "coherent and grounded" or "please reconnect to the server." The most magnetic people are the ones whose energy doesn't argue with their message. They're simply *coherent.*

Let me prove this point with what I witnessed at Starbucks a few weeks ago. I was standing in line behind a guy who was rehearsing a conversation under his breath. His jaw was tight, his shoulders were high, eyes were darting. Every molecule of him was either screaming "I'm about to get fired!" or "I'm about to propose!" When he got to the counter, he smiled big and said, "Hi! How are you?!" And the barista blinked twice, leaned back slightly, and said, "I'm...good?" I could hear her thoughts clear as day: *Sir, your aura is yelling at me.*

Good or bad, presence always leaks into the room. Even your latte knows when your energy is off.

To describe that same scene in a more nerdy way, inside our brains lives a secret empathy network called mirror neurons. Those are the unsung heroes of human connection—they fire when you perform an action *and* when you observe someone else doing it. They're why the barista leaned away from the on-the-verge-of-exploding customer and why you flinch when you see someone stub their toe. Mirror neurons are also the reason you start to mimic your friends' phrases without realizing it. Your brain is constantly scanning and syncing with others. It's running an unconscious command: "Copy energy, paste emotion."

That's why when someone calm walks in, you relax, but when someone anxious walks in, you brace yourself. And when someone walks in radiating "Monday and I are not on speaking terms," the whole room subconsciously lowers its vibration to match. Mirror neurons are your body's built-in empathy Wi-Fi that's downloading other people's emotional states whether you consciously subscribe to them or not.

The Science of Vibes (a.k.a. the "Room Read")

A few studies out of Princeton and UCLA found something wild: within thirty nine milliseconds, our brains can detect micro-expressions—tiny shifts in facial muscles that reveal emotional truth before a person even speaks. That's faster than a blink. Your body literally *feels* people before your brain can *think* about them. Which means that when you walk into a meeting, classroom, or first date, your nervous system has already taken attendance. It knows who's grounded, who's faking calm, and who's spiraling internally while pretending to love small talk.

Meanwhile, your mirror neurons *match* other people's energy. Your physiology syncs up with the emotional "leader" in the room, the one who's broadcasting the clearest frequency. That's why a calm leader can lower everyone's anxiety and why a panicked leader can turn a stable meeting into a collective meltdown faster than you can say "team huddle." Presence, then, isn't dominance. It's regulation leadership. It's about calibrating people, not controlling them.

I did my best to remember this when I walked into another high-stakes meeting years after my previous confidence disaster. Before I opened the door, I took three slow breaths and reminded myself, *My job isn't to impress. My job is to regulate.* When I walked in, I noticed the energy immediately: tight, impatient, and caffeine-dependent. Instead of matching it, though, I grounded—I slowed my tone, softened my shoulders, and sat still. Within two minutes, the volume of conversation dropped. The CFO leaned back in his chair. Someone actually smiled. In short, the room mirrored me. And that's the paradox of presence: the calmer you are, the louder your energy speaks.

This state of matching—when your breathing, heart rate, and emotions are in sync with others—is called physiological coherence. It's when your brain sends a signal of safety to everyone around you. People might not know why they trust you, but they *do*, because safety feels like truth. Presence might be known as a "soft skill," but even more importantly, it's a biological advantage. It's leadership on a frequency level.

We've all met that person who's trying to *look* confident. You know the type: their handshake lasts three seconds too long and their smile could power a small city. Their PowerPoint transitions include sparkles *and* sound effects. But biology can't fake safety—every muscle fiber, every micro-expression, every inhale is broadcasting one of two messages: either "I'm safe" or "I'm seeking safety." That's why the most magnetic people often *underperform* confidence. They anchor the room, they don't push energy into it. Their calmness is essentially saying, "You can relax now—the pilot knows how to fly this plane."

In the first ninety seconds of someone meeting you, they're silently wondering, *Do I feel comfortable around this person?* Then comes the congruence check: *Does what they say match what I'm feeling from them?* And last but not least comes the hierarchy read, when they wonder, *Is this person grounded enough to follow, or are they so reactive that I need to avoid them?* Essentially, they're detecting coherence alignment (or a lack thereof) between your tone, posture, and emotional state.

If your energy feels safe, people's brains shift into alpha waves (the "I trust you" zone). If your energy feels chaotic, their brains flip into beta waves (the "brace for impact" zone). Silence broadcasts, too. People can *feel* when someone's internally spiraling, even if their face says "I'm good." The room's first impression is entirely body to body, nervous system to nervous system, and that's why you can't talk your way into presence. You can only *regulate* your way into it.

The S.I.G.N.A.L. Method™: Your Presence Playbook

Now let's talk about your internal Wi-Fi upgrade, or what I call The S.I.G.N.A.L. Method™. It's a literal recalibration system, a way to broadcast grounded confidence no matter what chaos you're walking into. Because even though most people think presence is a talent, really, it's a signal chain, and you're either sending clarity or static. The S.I.G.N.A.L. Method™ is how you can reprogram that broadcast intentionally.

S: Self-Regulate Before You Communicate

Your nervous system is the bouncer of your emotional nightclub. If you're anxious, your body starts checking IDs and scanning for threats that don't exist. Before you speak, then, you must calm the bouncer. Take three breaths. Take a longer exhale. Make sure your shoulders are down. *BOOM!* Your prefrontal cortex (the logic part) will come back online. Now you're leading the conversation instead of just surviving it.

I: Intend the Outcome, Not the Impression

Most people walk into a room trying to look confident, but that's the wrong signal—your brain will interpret self-focus as danger. Instead of that inward focus, set an *outward* intention: "I'm here to connect," "I'm here to serve," "I'm here to learn." That single mental reframe shifts your physiology; your heart rate will lower, your empathy will rise, your tone will soften. Science calls this social orientation. I call it getting out of your own head.

G: Ground Physically in the Moment

You can't be mentally present if your body's in the past, so be here *now*. Plant your feet shoulder-width apart. Feel gravity. Uncross your arms. In short, broadcast stability. You can imagine roots running down your legs into the floor, too. Sounds poetic, but your vagus nerve loves that imagery. It tells your body, "We're safe here."

N: Notice the Room Before You Try to Lead It

Leaders who fail at presence try to take a room before they read it. They walk in broadcasting their agenda before they've scanned the vibe. But attunement precedes influence! Make eye contact with a few people first and notice their breathing pace, posture, and tone. Let yourself sync with them. This tiny act makes the group feel *seen*, and when people feel seen, they *follow*.

A: Align Words, Tone, and Energy

This is where authenticity lives. You can't say "I'm thrilled to be here" while blinking Morse code for "Send help." Speak more slowly. Match your pace to your feeling. If you're nervous, admit it with grace. Vulnerability and congruence are better than fake bravado every time. People trust truth, not polish.

L: Leave the Room Better Than You Found It

You don't need a TED Talk to make an impact—you just need to leave emotional oxygen behind. Ask yourself, "Will people feel smaller or seen after I leave?" That's legacy in real time. Presence is more about being *felt* than remembered.

When all of these six elements align, your signal stabilizes. You stop leaking insecurity and start transmitting coherence. You literally become a walking nervous system reset button. And people *feel* that. That's the paradox of presence: it's invisible, but unforgettable.

How To Practice the S.I.G.N.A.L. Method™ In Daily Life

Mastering presence isn't about being Zen 24/7, it's about micro-moments of regulation stacked over time. The goal is here is *recovery speed.* You're going to lose the signal at some point—the key is how fast you reconnect.

In Meetings

Most people sprint to fill silence because they're terrified of it, but silence is *power.* It tells the room, "I'm comfortable enough not to rush." That's social gravity in action; you bend the tempo around your calm. Try this: before you speak, take a beat longer than what feels normal. Let your breath finish before your sentence starts. You'll notice heads subtly tilt toward you. Why? Because humans equate stillness with stability. Silence is confidence with the volume turned down.

In Interviews

Forget rehearsing "perfect" answers. That's just anxiety doing karaoke. Instead, rehearse your *state of being.* Slow your breathing, soften your shoulders, and make eye contact with your interviewer like you're talking to a friend, not an FBI agent. Your nervous system becomes the message. Interviewers aren't going to remember your words, they're going to remember how they *felt* around you. Your goal is to demonstrate regulation under pressure.

In Relationships

Presence means listening slowly. It means *hearing* without composing your rebuttal mid-sentence. Most arguments aren't about who's right, they're about who's *regulated.* Try the three-second rule: when someone finishes talking, wait three seconds before you respond. It feels awkward at first, but that pause rewires everything. It tells the other person "I actually heard you" and tells your nervous system "We're not in danger."

In Leadership

Great leaders radiate coherence. They're not the loudest voice, but they are the most emotionally consistent one. When chaos hits, your team is scanning you for signals, and if you're frantic, they'll magnify that to the nth degree. If you're grounded, though, they'll match your calmness. That's real influence: *regulation by example.*

I guarantee you that every magnetic leader you've ever admired has mastered one ancient, underrated skill: they pause. They don't rush words to escape silence. They use silence to let their meaning land, and that calmness becomes the punctuation mark that people remember. That's because when speakers slow their delivery, the listener's brain switches from beta state (defensive, analytical) to alpha state (receptive, trusting). Pausing literally changes how others process your words. Silence is actually emotional white space, the thing that gives your message contours. When you hold silence comfortably, it tells the room, "I'm not afraid of stillness." And *that* is the sound of authority.

The Funny Side of Presence

Let's be honest: no amount of mindfulness can save you from real-life comedy. You can have the perfect energy and the most grounded breathing when you kick off a meeting...and then your AirPods connect to your kid's iPad blaring *Baby Shark.* You can be mid-speech when your dog decides to audition for Cirque du Soleil behind you on Zoom. Or worse, you freeze mid-presentation, forget your point, and blurt out, "I blacked out, but I think it went great."

Presence doesn't mean perfection, it means *grace under absurdity.* If you can laugh, breathe, and keep your signal stable through chaos, you've reached Level 10 Presence. Composure without humor is control. Composure with humor? *That's* mastery.

Besides, every room you walk into is just waiting for permission to calm down. When you enter grounded, congruent, and self-regulated, you become that permission slip. When you can maintain grace and humor in the most awkward of moments, your presence tells everyone's nervous system, "We're safe. We're seen. We can exhale." That's the ultimate broadcast. That's signal mastery.

WITHIN REACH TOOLKIT
The S.I.G.N.A.L. Method™ Checklist

Use this quick calibration before any high-stakes moment, be it an interview, a meeting, a keynote address, or a difficult conversation.

STEP	FOCUS	ASK YOURSELF	BIOLOGICAL SHIFT	RESULT
S	Self-regulate	"Am I calm or chaotic?"	Activates parasympathetic system	Nervous system coherence
I	Intend	"Why am I here, really?"	Shifts focus outward	Clarity over impression
G	Ground	"Am I anchored in my body?"	Stabilizes posture and breath	Confidence through embodiment
N	Notice	"What's the room's emotional temperature?"	Triggers empathy circuit	Connection before control
A	Align	"Do my words match my energy?"	Synchronizes tone and body language	Authentic comm-unication
L	Leave better	"Will they feel seen when I leave?"	Releases oxytocin in others	Lasting influence

Bonus Exercise: "Signal Resets in the Wild"

Whenever you feel your internal Wi-Fi drop:

1. **Stop.** Physically pause.
2. **Name it.** You can even say to yourself or others, "Signal weak recalibrating." (Humor helps.)
3. **Breathe out twice as long as you breathe in.**
4. **Reset your intention.** Ask yourself, "Who am I serving right now?"
5. **Reenter the moment.**

Do that five times a day and watch your baseline energy become bulletproof! And remember, presence isn't about being remembered, it's about being *felt*. You don't need to be the loudest, you just need to be *aligned*. Because when your signal is strong, words are secondary. The room already knows what you're broadcasting since your energy did the introduction. And somewhere, that confident version of you—the one you've been building piece by piece—just smirked and said, "Told you the Wi-Fi would connect."

When Presence Becomes Pull

Presence gets you noticed, but *gravity* is what keeps people close. Connection is what makes people want to stay. Even though the quiet chemistry created by presence (not to be confused with charisma) doesn't shout "Look at me!", somehow, everyone wants to lean closer anyway. Once your inner world starts resonating with your truth—once you carry peace that doesn't need proof—people feel it. They don't know why they trust you, why they listen, why they want to be around you, they just *do*. It's not manipulation, it's magnetism. It's the byproduct of integrity meeting alignment. Gravity is what happens when your life says *the same thing your mouth does.*

God designed influence to be felt before it's ever spoken. The pull of authenticity, humility, and genuine care can move people more than strategy ever could. Sure, presence gets you in the door, but gravity—holy, human, heart-centered gravity—is what turns encounters into impact.

CHAPTER 8

Social Gravity—Why Some People Just Pull You In

You ever meet someone who just *has* it? Not the loud kind of "it," not the motivational-speaker-in-a-blazer energy, but that quiet gravitational pull that makes you want to lean in. It's like their soul is speaking fluent peace. In short, they have social gravity—their authenticity bends space around them until people naturally orbit their truth.

Psychologists call this limbic resonance, or the mirroring of emotional states between humans. The Bible calls it anointing, having a presence that draws other people in before you even say a word. Either way, the effect's the same: people don't remember what you said, they remember how you made their nervous system feel. Congruence is what lies at the heart of this kind of presence, a.k.a. you being more fully *you.* When alignment turns into attraction, your presence starts pulling the right people, opportunities, and divine collisions straight into your orbit.

I came across this phenomenon when I was at a networking event and met a guy who somehow convinced forty adults to stand in a loose circle while he told a story about...losing his AirPods. That was it. No billion-dollar idea, no heroic comeback story. Just AirPods. And yet everyone was captivated—laughing, nodding, leaning in like the guy was handing out free Teslas and emotional validation. Meanwhile, I was standing there holding my mini-cheesecake bite and trying to figure out how this man had the gravitational pull of a small moon.

Social gravity is the unseen current of human connection, and it might just be the most underrated professional skill you'll ever assemble. If confidence was the furniture filling the room, this is the power outlet that electrifies it. You're either the person whom people orbit inside of that room or the one they politely escape while muttering, "Great catching up!"

Charisma Isn't DNA, It's Data

We love to say, "That person's just naturally charismatic," but science begs to disagree. Like confidence, charisma is built, not born. It's a learnable formula of warmth, competence, and congruence: warmth ("I like you") + competence ("I trust you") + congruence ("You mean what you say") = charisma. Miss one, and the whole recipe curdles like the protein shake I forgot I left in my backpack last week. If you're warm but not competent, then you're adorable but forgettable. Competent but not warm? Impressive but intimidating. But all three? Ah—*that's* when everything clicks and people relax. And relaxed people lean in. That's gravity. That's also cognitive coherence: our brains crave predictable patterns, and when someone's energy is consistent, we subconsciously think, "I can trust this."

I came across this personified in the form of Nina, a twenty-two-year-old intern who made executives laugh. During her first big meeting, the VP's slide deck froze mid-presentation. The tension could've powered a Tesla. Nina leaned in and said, "It's okay—just call it Version 2026."

The room cracked up. The VP smiled. Tension evaporated. No one remembered the glitch. Everyone remembered Nina, though, because when humor is timed right, it's emotional hospitality. It signals, "You're safe here," and safety is irresistible. Nina's levity didn't just make people laugh, it made people *breathe.* That's what real influence feels like.

Charisma can be tricky to build, though—it's too easy to fall into the trap of chasing approval and accidentally repelling people. What was true in childhood is still true in adulthood: the harder we try to be liked, the less liked we are. Trying to convince other people to like us instead of just connecting with them oozes insecurity. People feel when we're auditioning for approval.

The good news is that you don't need to perform likability, you need to practice congruence. Just be genuinely curious! Every meaningful interaction releases oxytocin, the trust hormone, but oxytocin *only* floods the system when connection is real. Fake enthusiasm? Spam folder. Over polished networking? LinkedIn invite denied. No authenticity → no oxy-tocin → no gravity. That's why the most magnetic people rarely try to impress you—instead, they just make you feel safe enough to drop your own mask. That's gravity in motion.

The P.U.L.L. Method™: How to Build Social Gravity

Magnetic people don't push energy outward, they pull others in through alignment. People *feel* the genuine connection.

FORCE	WHAT IT MEANS	CORE QUESTION
P: Presence	Be fully there; people can feel divided attention.	"Am I actually here?"
U: Understanding	Make people feel seen.	"Have I made space for them to be real?"
L: Levity	Use humor and warmth to lower resistance.	"Did I make this moment lighter?"
L: Leadership	Guide, don't grab. Influence through stability.	"Am I grounding or grasping?"

The Mechanics of Magnetism

In a world where everyone's half-listening and half-refreshing, full attention is rarer than a verified LinkedIn influencer who's actually humble. Which is why presence is about being anchored. Most people live entirely in their heads: having anxious inner monologues, putting on mental rehearsals, getting tangled in phantom debates with imaginary critics. So before every conversation, ask yourself, "Am I in my body or in my head?" Because when you're truly present, others feel it viscer-ally—the vagus nerve (which runs from the brainstem to the gut) picks up on micro-cues of safety or danger.

You can tell someone else's body "You're okay here" through calm breathing, a relaxed tone, and genuine eye contact. In essence, the more present you are—the more anchored you are—the less you need to *do*. Presence itself becomes magnetism.

Unfortunately, most people don't listen—they reload. Rather than being present, they're buffering, just waiting for their turn to drop a hot take. And because they're not cultivating active empathy and therefore not trying to actively understand what's being said, they're not going to make the speaker feel understood. *That* means nobody's brain is going to release oxytocin or dopamine, a trust-reward combo that would have otherwise literally rewired the relationship.

When you're the one on the listening end of a conversation, don't let that trust-reward opportunity slip by! Ask yourself, "Am I listening to *respond* or to *understand*?" If it's the latter, enjoy the natural rush of connection that follows.

I witnessed an intern—who tended to be a bit nervous—save a pitch during a high-stakes client presentation thanks to her awareness and understanding of the client's body language. Nobody else noticed the crossed arms or the tense shoulders or the glazing-over eyes, but she did. And while the senior manager kept talking at the client, she quietly slid the manager a note: "Pause. Ask what's missing."

He did. The client blinked, smiled, and said, "Honestly? You're saying what you do, but not what it does for us." The conversation pivoted. They won the contract. All thanks to the intern's awareness. Because real understanding doesn't come from knowledge, it comes from *noticing*.

Humor is another facet of understanding—it's empathy in disguise. It's about creating exhale moments. When people laugh, they stop performing. Their prefrontal cortex—the part that filters, censors, and self-protects—loosens its grip. Connection lives in those microseconds where we forget to be impressive and where we let ourselves laugh. Science backs this up: laughter increases dopamine (motivation), serotonin (stability), and endorphins (bonding). It literally tells your brain, "I belong here." Fortunately, you don't need to be the office comedian to bring humor into the room—you just need to be human enough to lighten the weight.

That said, similar to likability, the more we push for the laugh, the less likely we are to receive it. Years ago, a husband-and-wife comedy duo had a recurring show that would always close with the husband asking the wife for a cup of tea, which would cause a huge roar from the crowd. Well, after a dozen shows or so, they stopped getting the laugh. Coming off stage after that happening for the third time, the husband asked the wife, "What's going on?!" The wife looked at her husband and said, "Before you would ask for tea, but now you're asking for a laugh..."

Authenticity and truth have to be at the center of humor, or those in the audience will see through the ruse and not laugh. Humor = honesty.

Generating P.U.L.L.

When you have all four elements of the P.U.L.L. Method™, the sum is greater than the parts. **P**resence gives safety. **U**nderstanding builds trust. **L**evity builds rapport. **L**eadership sustains peace. Together, they make an exponential impact, which is why you don't want to overlook any of the elements.

Think of every conversation like an orbit. Your energy—your PULL—determines whether people drift closer or break away. Social gravity starts with emotional congruence: the alignment between what you *feel*, what you *think*, and what you *express*. And just like you'd go to the gym to practice better mastery of physical gravity—i.e., lifting things—you can practice generating greater social gravity, too.

The 5-Second Reset

Before any interview, first date, or Thanksgiving (a.k.a. emotional Cross-Fit), run this calibration:

1. **Exhale slowly.** Tell your body it's safe. The exhale triggers your parasympathetic nervous system (the chill zone).
2. **Drop your shoulders.** You're probably carrying more tension than a bad Wi-Fi connection.
3. **Ask** "What energy does this room need from me?" Not "How can I prove myself?," but "How can I stabilize?"
4. **Choose calm curiosity.** Curiosity turns fear into data.
5. **Enter quietly powerful.** Gravity never yells.

That's your social gravity warm-up.

Auditing Your Energy (a.k.a. Your Magnetism)

People are attracted to people with a calm, grounded presence. They're also drawn to people who are competent. Not surprisingly, in an article in *Harvard Business Review*, the authors found that being both competent *and* likable accelerates promotions, increases collaboration, and even improves perceived intelligence. But! Beware of confusing likability with people-pleasing. People-pleasers bend; likable leaders *center*. They make others feel seen without disappearing, and doors open faster for people whom others like to root for.

Likable people make others feel safe being themselves, and *that's* a competitive advantage money can't buy. If your relationships feel heavy, awkward, or one-sided, you probably have a likability calibration issue, not a compatibility issue. You can check this by running a quick diagnostic:

1. **After you leave a conversation, how do people feel?** Lighter or drained?
2. **Do you dominate space or create it?** There's a difference between being heard and hogging the air.
3. **Do people open up or shut down around you?** Openness is feedback.
4. **Do you make others feel safe enough to be imperfect?** Because vulnerability only shows up when people feel protected.

This is the emotional version of checking your car's alignment. You may be going forward, but if your wheels (intentions, tone, attention) aren't aligned—or if you aren't coming across as likable—you'll still drift off the road. Remember, your energy is your reputation. People might forget your words, but they'll *never* forget how their nervous system felt around you. The most magnetic people transmit safety consistently. That's why the best communicators feel like home even as they're holding everybody accountable.

Every interaction has two timelines: the halo, which is how people feel while they're with you, and the echo, which is what they say after you leave. The halo is the experience; the echo is the story. The quiet leader who steadies chaos leaves a calm echo. The thoughtful listener leaves a gratitude echo. The humorist who makes people breathe leaves a lightness echo.

People rarely describe these perceptions out loud, but their decisions are built on them. You get recommended for being safe to succeed with, for being grounded. Fortunately, during every conversation, every meeting, and every handshake, you have the opportunity to be 1% more grounding than the environment around you, and that 1% compounds—over a year, it becomes a gravitational field.

When you're calm, people borrow your calm. When you're excited, they borrow your spark. When you're grounded, they find their footing. Through every sigh, pause, and tone, you're teaching others how to feel around you.

Of course, you can't build magnetism—the halo and the echo—overnight. You train it through repetition, awareness, and recovery. In that spirit, here's your daily workout plan:

- **Practice deliberate presence.** Put your phone down for one full conversation each and every day.
- **Name emotions out loud.** Saying "I'm nervous" out loud reduces its charge by 40%.
- **Use micro-humor.** You can go with a light tease, a smile, or calling out the awkwardness: "Well, this meeting started out spicy."
- **Give micro-validations.** Every time you say something like "That makes sense" or "I hear you" or "Good point," you're making tiny deposits into the trust account.
- **Anchor with curiosity.** Replace judgment with "Tell me more."
- **End on uplift.** Leave a residue of warmth: "It was great talking to you."

These actions may sound simple, but small energy choices become identity patterns. You can't fake social gravity. You have to *become* the force that pulls people closer.

> ## WITHIN REACH TOOLKIT
> ### The P.U.L.L. Method™

Now let's turn the science into a system you can actually use—specifically, with your PULL.

P: Presence

What it is: The art of being fully in the moment, emotionally, mentally, and physically.

Why it works: Presence signals safety; your nervous system teaches others how to feel.

Micro-practices:

- Take three deep breaths before entering any room.
- Drop your shoulders. Loosen your jaw.
- Make eye contact long enough to be felt, but not long enough to be weird.
- Speak 10% slower than you think you should.

Cue: "I am here, not proving I belong here."

U: Understanding

What it is: Listening to *understand*, not to respond.

Why it works: Being seen triggers oxytocin, building trust, and openness.

Micro-practices:

- Mirror what you hear: "Sounds like that's been tough."
- Ask follow-up questions: "What made you feel that way?"
- Validate feelings before fixing problems.

Cue: "They don't need my answers, they need my attention."

L: Levity

What it is: The ability to add lightness without losing depth.
Why it works: Humor releases tension and resets the nervous system.

Micro-practices:

- Tell a light self-own to humanize yourself.
- Use shared humor—don't be sarcastic at the expense of others.
- Smile from empathy, not performance.

Cue: "If I can help them exhale, I've already led."

L: Leadership

What it is: Grounded energy that regulates others without demanding control.
Why it works: Calm is contagious; anxiety multiplies faster.

Micro-practices:

- Breathe before speaking.
- Don't match chaos, neutralize it.
- Lead by tone and pace, not volume.

Cue: "Be the calm that recalibrates the room."

Quick Recap Formula

Presence creates *safety.*
Understanding creates *trust.*
Levity creates *openness.*
Leadership creates *stability.*
Together, they form gravity.

Bonus Tool: The Halo + Echo Tracker

Each week, ask yourself two reflection questions:

1. Halo: "How did people feel while I was there?"
2. Echo: "What did they say after I left?"

Write it down. Notice patterns. Adjust accordingly. That's emotional awareness with metrics.

WITHIN REACH TOOLKIT SUMMARY
Social Gravity Edition

Influence isn't about being the loudest voice, it's about being the clearest frequency. The world is already deafened by egos, filters, and performance energy! People crave *peace,* not perfection, and when you walk in calm, congruent, and kind, you become that peace. Everyone feels it.

Don't chase attention—bend it quietly, confidently, and completely. Be the gravity, not the noise.

SKILL	DAILY PRACTICE	BRAIN EFFECT	EMOTIONAL ROI
Presence	Take a three-breath reset before any meeting	Activates para-sympathetic system	Calm energy = credibility
Understanding	Practice reflective listening	Boosts oxyto-cin and trust	Makes others feel safe
Levity	Use shared humor/self-own	Releases dopamine and serotonin	Lowers tension, raises connection
Leadership	Have a grounded tone and a slow pace	Stabilizes mirror neurons	Regulates the room
Energy audit	Reflect weekly	Increases self-awareness	Sustains authenticity over time

When you leave a room, people shouldn't just remember your résumé, they should remember how their heartbeat slowed when you spoke. That's not luck, that's design. *That's* social gravity.

When Gravity Meets Calling

The more you study connection, the more you'll realize it isn't random. In fact, it's choreography. God uses us like magnets, pulling us toward places and purposes we hadn't even known existed yet. Some relationships are assignments. Some are accelerators. And some are just mirrors that remind of us who we really are when we start to forget.

That's the secret to social gravity: it doesn't just draw people to you, it draws *you* back to your purpose. Every divine collision, every "chance" encounter, every conversation that changed your direction—none of it was coincidence. It was coordination. Because before you can light someone else's path, you have to remember where your own spark came from. Before you can inspire, you have to go back to the moment when *you* were inspired. The place where potential met calling and God whispered, "This is where your story begins." The moment the light turned on and you thought, *Hey, this journey isn't about chasing connection! It's about following the flame that first connected me to my purpose.*

CHAPTER 9

The Faith, Fire, and Fortune of a Quiet Beginning

Every story has a beginning, but not every beginning feels like a beginning when you're living it. Sometimes it just feels like an ordinary Tuesday that accidentally turns into destiny. My story started somewhere between frustration and faith, in a season where nothing made sense and everything felt too small for what was growing inside me.

Looking back, I realize that's usually how God lights the fuse: not with fireworks, but with friction. You pray for clarity, and He gives you discomfort. You ask for direction, and He gives you a dead end that forces you to turn. That's not punishment, that's positioning.

The moment that changed everything didn't arrive wrapped in angelic lighting or cinematic music—it came disguised as work, as "just another day." As the moment I stopped waiting for life to hand me purpose and decided to create meaning right where I was standing. Because sparks *create* perfect conditions, they don't wait for them. And for me, what started as a tiny flicker of "Maybe there's more than this" became the fire that shaped every chapter after.

The Express Lane to Retail Infamy

I got my first real job in college at Express because I needed money. College textbooks were expensive, gas was expensive, and Taco Bell's "cheap menu" was getting less cheap by the week. So, I did what any broke college student would do: I got a job folding clothes for minimum wage and maximum humility. If you've ever worked retail, you know that folding clothes is 80% of the job, pretending to look busy is 15%, and mentally rehearsing your two-weeks' notice speech is the other 5%.

But apparently, I was *terrible* at folding clothes. Like, impressively bad. Picasso-level abstract folding. My boss, bless her patient retail soul, realized that if I kept folding, we'd lose more shirts than we sold. So, she said, "John, why don't we...find something else for you to do?" Translation: "Before we fire you, let's see if we can redirect your chaos."

It was the post-Thanksgiving retail apocalypse—more commonly known as the holiday season—when every checkout line wrapped around the store twice and emotions were hanging by a thread (usually a cashmere one). Amid the chaos, my boss decided to weaponize my biggest flaw, which was talking too much: she stationed me in front of the line to entertain people while they waited to pay. Imagine a college kid new to the powers of caffeine and not enough supervision doing crowd work at the checkout line... That was me.

I started talking to everyone, making jokes, guessing people's favorite cologne, inventing fake backstories for shoppers. I treated that Express line like it was *The Tonight Show.* Some customers loved it. Some smiled politely. A few probably wished they'd gone to Abercrombie. But one woman, one random older woman, would change everything.

She walked up with a smile that looked like she already knew something I didn't. I greeted her with my usual line: "Welcome to Express! What's your return policy on patience today?"

She chuckled and said, "Young man, can I ask you a question?"

"Of course," I said. "Unless it's about The Kennedy Assassination, we don't have that kind of time." She laughed, shook her head, and said, "No, no... Have you ever thought about being an actor?"

And in that exact moment, in between the smell of cologne testers and the sound of the register beeping, something inside me *moved.* And it was not the Taco Bell, for a change. This was different—this was a *spark.*

It was like someone had flipped a switch I didn't even know existed. One second I was a retail employee joking my way through a shift, and the next, I was suddenly aware of this electric pull toward something bigger, something that felt like *home*, even though I'd never been there.

The Spark

It's funny how one sentence from a stranger can light up an entire map you didn't even know existed. When she asked that question, it wasn't just about acting, it was about *possibility*. About permission to imagine a version of myself that wasn't stuck behind a cash register or buried in engineering textbooks. In that moment, I decided—no, I *knew*—that I was going to move to Los Angeles and chase the spark.

Did I have a plan? Nope. Did I have money? Also nope. Did I know anyone in L.A.? Not unless you count the cast of *Friends*. But what I *did* have was a feeling, that rare kind of internal lightning that tells you, "This isn't random. Pay attention."

Looking back now, I realize that moment wasn't just about dreaming. It was my first conscious act of betting on myself. That spark didn't just push me toward Hollywood, it built the foundation of how I'd approach every big decision after that. At the time, I thought I was chasing fame, but really, I was chasing *alignment.* I was following something that made me feel alive.

It's easy to call that being naïve. But naïveté is often just courage without experience. That impulse—to chase the unknown, to commit before you're ready, to do the thing that doesn't make sense yet—that's faith in disguise. It's not loud. It's not polished. But it's the same force that would one day drive me through hard careers, big challenges, and impossible projects. Plus, the biggest pivot of my life was still on the horizon, and I would need every ounce of faith I had.

That random Tuesday night at Express taught me something no class-room ever could: sometimes the moment that changes everything shows up wearing a smile and holding a shopping bag. And when it does, pay attention. Because that little spark might just be the pilot light for your purpose.

Step 1: Spot the pattern break.

Notice what makes your brain sit up. A compliment that lands differently, a conversation that gives you goosebumps, a subject that makes you lose track of time—those are all sparks trying to introduce themselves.

Step 2: Name the feeling, not the outcome.

Instead of asking "What job could this lead to?" ask "What part of this made me feel alive?" You're tracking energy, not titles.

Step 3: Run the 30-second test.

If you can talk about something for 30 seconds without checking your phone or apologizing for caring, it's worth exploring. Curiosity is the brain's earliest form of commitment.

Step 4: Build micro-momentum.

Do one ridiculously small thing that moves you toward your spark: Google a class, send a DM, write a note in your phone. Action releases more dopamine, which reinforces your new identity loop.

Step 5: Collect your sparks.

Keep a running list (yes, actual notes on your phone) titled "Sparks." Every time you feel that internal lightning, jot it down. Over time, you'll start seeing themes, and those themes will point directly toward purpose.

Bottom line: Sparks aren't random—they're neurological breadcrumbs leading you back to yourself. The trick isn't finding them, it's trusting them long enough to follow where they lead.

The Reachable Moment

When I look back at that day at Express, I realize that woman didn't *give* me a dream, she just reminded me I was allowed to have one. That's what a spark is: a moment of recognition that who you *could be* just brushed shoulders with who you *are.* If you're lucky enough to feel it, don't over-think it! Feed it. Follow it. Fold fewer shirts.

There's a reason that kind of moment hits like a caffeine dart straight to the soul, and neuroscientists call it dopaminergic tagging. It's when your brain marks an experience as important by flooding it with emotion and novelty. Think of it as your nervous system highlighting a page in your life and scribbling in the margins: "Remember this! It matters."

When that woman asked if I'd ever thought about acting, my brain registered it as a pattern break, something unexpected that jolted me out of autopilot. Pattern breaks activate the brain's salience network, which basically decides what's worth paying attention to. Once that network lights up, dopamine rushes in, and suddenly an ordinary moment feels extraordinary. That's what a spark really is: a surge of chemical curiosity that says, "Hey, this could be something special!"

The problem is that most people dismiss a moment like that. They logic it away, telling themselves it's random or unrealistic. But ignoring those neural nudges is like not bothering to pick up your phone when purpose is calling.

Every major pivot starts with a tiny physiological whisper: your heartbeat quickens, your energy spikes, and your brain starts building stories around a new possibility. That's by design—the spark isn't meant to stay contained! It's meant to travel, person to person, moment to moment, through ordinary interactions that carry extraordinary weight.

As I followed that flame myself, I learned something critical: God rarely reveals the whole path at once. He does reveal the next person, though, and that's where the story goes next. Fires that change our lives don't grow in silence, they grow in connection. That's where networking— *real* networking, not just the corporate hand-out-your-business-card kind—begins.

CHAPTER 10

Why Real Connections Start Where Most People Never Look

If you had told me that half of the biggest doors in my life would open because of random conversations, awkward small talk, and coffee-shop coincidences, I would've laughed, prayed for your discernment, and gone back to my spreadsheet. But that's the thing about divine networking: it rarely looks strategic in real time. It looks more like obedience disguised as accident.

I'm guessing that for you, too, just about every connection that changed your trajectory started out as an ordinary moment wrapped around an extraordinary nudge. A chance encounter you almost skipped. A conversation you almost talked yourself out of. A stranger who somehow knew the next step before you did. This fortunate tendency is serendipity bias—it's the brain's way of noticing meaning where others see randomness. Faith calls it favor, God's way of proving He's better at LinkedIn than you'll ever be.

But even though you can't plan for holy collisions, you absolutely can *position* yourself to receive them. When you follow the spark, you network through connecting purpose as opposed to people. Case in point: I accidentally built a network one unplanned "yes" at a time even though for years, I thought that networking was corporate code for "pretend to care long enough that someone offers you a job." Every mixer I went to felt like speed dating for business cards—everyone had that "I love small talk" smile plastered on while they were scanning the room like sharks looking for the one person who looked more desperate than they did. Meanwhile, I was usually the guy in the corner pretending to check my phone.

I'd always thought networking was about *getting* something: a job, an introduction, a miracle. But the more I studied psychology and the more I watched how the right people seemed to "just attract" opportunity, the more I realized I had it completely backwards. Networking isn't about collecting people, it's about showing up for them; it's not about "who you know," it's about "who feels known when they're around you." When you flip that equation, the "net" finally starts working.

Maya Angelou probably said it best when she said, "People will forget what you said, they will forget what you did, but they will never forget how you made them feel." Make people "feel" something, and they'll do anything they can to get you in front of the right people so they can "feel" something, too.

The Moment It Clicked

A few years back, I landed a rare one-on-one meeting with a high-ranking executive, the kind of person who's normally booked out three fiscal years in advance. He'd been a panelist for a job I had interviewed for, and somehow, we clicked enough that he said, "Let's grab coffee." Cue panic.

I remember thinking, *What on earth could I possibly bring to the table that's going to add value to this guy's life?* At that point, my biggest accomplishment was learning how to make my thumb appear to come off my hand. Not exactly Fortune 500 material.

Fifteen minutes into the conversation, I was still mentally scrambling for something insightful to say when he started talking about his kids. They were heading off to college soon, and he was both proud and terrified, like most parents feel when they're standing at the edge of that cliff.

And there was my moment: not a chance to impress him, but a chance to *serve* him. So, I asked questions. Listened. Got genuinely curious about what his kids were studying, where they were headed, and how they were adjusting. A few days later, I mailed each of them a handwritten letter and included two of my favorite books. That was it. No pitch. No thinking, *Hope this gets me a callback.* Just a simple gesture that said, "Hey, I see you."

A week later, I got an email from the exec thanking me for my thoughtfulness. More importantly, that conversation started a relationship that's still active to this day. I didn't send those books to "get" anything. I sent them because I'd finally learned the secret: when you stop networking to be noticed and start connecting to *notice others*, God starts doing the heavy lifting for you.

A quick aside to talk about the word itself: net + work. A net can't function if it's made of one strand. It's the connection points, the *links*, that make it strong. That means networking isn't just who you know, it's the collective web of people you've lifted, encouraged, and inspired over time. That's the work part—you have to tend to the net, checking for breaks, repairing weak spots, strengthening ties. Not because you're trying to catch something, but because one day, that same net might catch *you.*

Why Reciprocity Changes Everything

When we think of networking as a game of extraction instead of exchange, then someone's always left depleted and the whole experience starts to feel transactional instead of transformational. That's because reciprocity is the oxygen of relationships. Without it, even the most well-intentioned connections suffocate over time. But here's a basic fact to remember: reciprocity doesn't mean keeping score, it means keeping energy in motion. It's a two-way current of value that doesn't have to look equal to be balanced. Sometimes you offer advice; sometimes you listen. Sometimes your only contribution is making someone laugh after a brutal week. That counts, too. Value doesn't have to be symmetrical to be meaningful.

Psychologists call it this phenomenon the reciprocity loop—when one person gives or helps, it activates the brain's reward center in *both* people. That shared dopamine hit tells both people's nervous systems, "This person is safe. You can trust them." That's why generosity feels so good. It's not just moral, it's *neurological.* Spiritually, it's even deeper. When you show up to pour into someone else without expecting a return, you create what I call divine momentum. God tends to fill the gaps you create by serving others: you step into someone's need, and somehow yours gets met in a way you couldn't have planned.

The reciprocity loop is why the people who seem the "luckiest" in their careers often aren't the loudest or most connected—they're the ones who keep giving long after giving stops being convenient. They build networks of people who *want* to work for them and with them because their energy has already worked for others. If you take nothing else from this section, take this: reciprocity doesn't start when someone helps you back, it starts the moment you decide to help them first. It's not karma, it's chemistry, character, and calling, all playing on the same team.

And yes, sometimes you'll pour into people who will never pour back. That's okay. You weren't investing in *them*, you were investing in *who you become* when you choose to stay generous. That's the kind of ROI that outlasts résumés and outperforms luck. Although that said, sometimes you'll pour into someone and hear nothing for years. Then one random day, your phone rings. "Hey, you probably don't remember me, but you helped me out once…" And suddenly, your act of generosity from 2017 is back with interest.

That's *divine compound interest.* Every act of service, every handwritten note, every moment you showed up for someone with no agenda—all of that is being stored somewhere in God's algorithm. And when the timing aligns, the doors that open will feel like coincidences. But they're not—they're earned connections. You can't predict the return. You just have to trust the process.

Here's something else to keep in mind: you don't need to have it all figured out to help someone else. In fact, sometimes the most powerful thing you can do is help from a place of need yourself. When you give while you're still struggling, it signals something rare: abundance without evidence. It's like saying, "Even though I don't have much, I still have something to give." And that kind of energy multiplies fast.

From a neuroscience standpoint, giving also triggers oxytocin, a.k.a. the "trust hormone." That combined with a dopamine release is why situations where you help someone else always leave *you* feeling lighter, too—your brain is literally thanking you for being a decent human. It's in those exact moments of giving, when you least feel equipped, that God tends to do His best work.

The Lost Art of Saying "Thank You"

There's something wildly powerful about two little words we rush past every day: thank you. In a world that's mastered the art of the thumbs-up emoji, genuine gratitude has become a rare currency. And just like any rare commodity, the less often that people use it, the higher its value becomes. Once upon a time, we wrote thank-you notes on actual paper, with pens, stamps, and cursive so illegible it looked like an exorcism. Now, we fire off "thx!" between Zoom calls and call that making a connection.

But actually telling somebody "Thank you!" is a different matter altogether. That's because when gratitude is *felt* and *shown*, it lowers cortisol, boosts serotonin, and increases feelings of belonging. In other words, it literally changes your body chemistry to make you *and* the person you thank happier and healthier. It's like free therapy accompanied by postage.

Let me tell you, I've never met a single person who hadn't been keeping a heartfelt thank-you note somewhere in their desk, drawer, or inbox. Even the most stoic executives have that *one* card they pull out on bad days to remind themselves that they matter. Handwritten thank-you notes are basically emotional time capsules—they freeze a moment of kindness and make it permanent.

Here's a real-world example of the power of thank-you notes: I once sent a thank-you card to someone who'd given me just ten minutes of her time. Nothing fancy, just a few lines about how her advice had shifted my perspective. Two years later, that same person called me out of the blue to offer me a project. She said, "I kept your card on my desk because it reminded me why I love mentoring." *That's* the quiet power of gratitude: it stays in the room long after you've left.

So, let's bring "thank you" back, analog-style! Try this:

- Once a month, handwrite a thank-you card to someone who's impacted you, even slightly.
- Don't overthink it. Write three sentences max:
  1. What they did.
  2. Why it mattered.
  3. How it made you feel.
- Sign it. Mail it. Move on.

No hashtags. No humblebrags. Just humanity. Because here's the psychology of it: the act of writing forces you to slow down and *feel* gratitude, not just perform it. And people can sense that authenticity in the ink, even subconsciously.

God designed gratitude as a feedback loop for joy. When you express it, you don't just bless someone else, you remind your own spirit that abundance still exists. And those who practice thankfulness end up attracting more reasons to be thankful. It's not a trick of luck, it's alignment. In an age of AI, algorithms, and automated replies, the handwritten thank-you card might be the most disruptive technology left. Because no app on earth can compete with the feeling of being *seen*.

Networking for Introverts

Let's address the elephant in your nervous system. When introverts hear "networking," they immediately want to fake having a dentist appointment. But here's the good news: introverts are *built* for meaningful networking. They just need to stop trying to network like extroverts.

If you're introverted, your power is depth, not volume. You don't need to talk to fifty people—you just need to make one person feel like they're the only one in the room. Here's your playbook:

1. Redefine success.

Don't measure success by the number of contacts. Measure it by quality of your conversations.

2. Pre-research your environment.

If you're walking into an event, identify two or three people ahead of time you'd genuinely love to meet. When you know why you're there, your anxiety has a mission.

3. Use the question-then-quiet method.

Ask something ("What's been the most fun project you've worked on this year?") and then *shut up and listen.* Listening is your superpower.

4. Follow up in writing.

Introverts tend to shine in reflection. A thoughtful message afterward can be more memorable than any in-person chat.

Networking for Extroverts

Extroverts, you are the human equivalent of espresso shots—you bring life to any room. But here's your Achilles' heel: sometimes you're *so busy talking* that people leave remembering your energy but not your value. If that's you, here's how to harness your gift without draining the room:

1. Talk less, anchor more.

Every conversation needs a landing point, a moment where the other person feels seen. Ask one meaningful follow-up question for every story you tell.

2. Learn to exit gracefully.

You don't have to stay until awkward silence settles in. End with energy: "This was great chatting! I'll let you keep mingling, but I'd love to follow up."

3. Be the connector.

Your superpower is breadth. Use it. Introduce people to each other. It's the fastest way to build goodwill without dominating the spotlight.

But no matter whether you're an introvert or an extrovert, the most important networking truth is simple: you don't need a network to start one. Start by giving what you *wish* you had. When you encourage someone else to chase their dream, you're rehearsing your own breakthrough. When you share someone's post or recommend their work, you're telling the universe, "I believe in abundance." That energy comes back multiplied. Always. Because connection—real connection—starts from generosity.

The C.A.S.T. Framework

We're not leaving this topic without a toolkit! Every interaction you have is a line cast into the unknown. Some days you reel in a mentor; some days you wind up with awkward silence. Either way, though, you learn how to throw better. Here's how to CAST with purpose:

C is for Curiosity: The Dopamine Doorway

Ask emotion-sparking questions like "What's been surprisingly fun about your work lately?" Curiosity fuels connection more than confidence ever will.

A is for Authenticity: The Oxytocin Trigger

Drop the armor and share something real: "I was so nervous before this event that I practiced smiling in the mirror." People love honesty more than polish.

S is for Service: The Reciprocity Magnet

Look for one way to make the other person's life easier, even if it's just an introduction, a link, or a kind word. Service builds momentum.

T is for Time-On-Target: The Memory Multiplier

Follow up without being weird: "Hey, that tip you gave me actually worked! Appreciate you!" Gratitude compounds over time.

Psychologist Richard Wiseman once studied so-called "lucky" people. Turns out they weren't lucky, they were *open.* They smiled more, asked more questions, said yes to coffee invites, and followed up. In other words, they made themselves available for blessing. That's what I call behavioral faith. It's trusting that if you keep planting seeds with kindness, consistency, and curiosity, something will bloom eventually. You can't control *when* it happens, but you can control whether you're in position when it does.

In my own life, every major opportunity has come from one of two things:

1. A small act of kindness I almost didn't do.
2. A conversation I didn't realize mattered.

When you make helping someone else get ahead the focus of your networking, somehow, you'll get pulled forward in the process, too. When you show up to help others—even when you feel underqualified, tired, or unsure—you create conditions for divine reciprocity. (I think of that as the divine equation.) The net starts to work. And you realize that maybe you didn't *accidentally* network your way into everything after all. Maybe you were just being faithful and the universe was keeping score.

WITHIN REACH TOOLKIT
The New Rules of Networking

1. The Networking Reframe

Before we dive into action steps, let's reset the entire premise: networking isn't about who can help you, it's about who *you* can help right now. When you show up with curiosity, generosity, and faith that provision flows through people rather than positions, everything changes.

Reflection Prompt

Who in your current orbit could use encouragement, connection, or opportunity right now, even if you're not in a position of power? Write down three names. Don't overthink it. Who are they, what might they need, and how could you help them? Even the smallest way to help counts.

2. The Reciprocity Equation: Generosity → Trust → Opportunity

The universe (and your nervous system) are wired to reward reciprocity. It's not transactional, it's energetic. Try doing these things on a weekly basis:

- ✓ Comment thoughtfully on someone's post.
- ✓ Introduce two people who should know each other.
- ✓ Share a resource, not a résumé.
- ✓ Say "thank you" like you mean it.

Reflection Prompt

When was the last time someone went out of their way for you and have you reciprocated yet? If not, what's one small way you can close that loop this week?

3. The Lost Art of Saying "Thank You"

Gratitude is social superglue: it closes the loop and keeps the oxygen relationship flowing. You can literally change someone's brain chemistry with a handwritten card! Which brings us to your micro-challenge of writing one thank-you card this month. Keep it short, but be sure to include:

1. What they did.
2. Why it mattered.
3. How it made you feel.

Bonus: Take a photo of the envelope before you mail it as proof that you're building legacy one stamp at a time.

4. The C.A.S.T. Framework (Networking Edition)

Every conversation is a line cast into the unknown, so here's your playbook for throwing those lines like a pro.

	PRINCIPLE	WHY IT WORKS	MICRO-ACTION
C	Curiosity	Triggers dopamine; makes connection fun, not forced	Ask something that makes them think or smile ("What's something you've learned the hard way this year?")
A	Authenticity	Activates oxytocin; builds safety	Share one small imperfection ("I still get nervous in meetings, too.")
S	Service	Starts the reciprocity loop	Offer one small way to make their life easier (intro, link, resource, etc.)
T	Time-on-target	Builds consistency; compounds goodwill	Follow up every 90 days with gratitude, not greed

5. The Energy Audit

Connection should feel expansive, not exhausting. After every interaction, ask:

- Did this conversation leave me energized or drained?
- Would future me thank present me for saying yes to this coffee chat?

If you feel drained, that's a red flag. If you feel inspired, that's your room.

Faith Reflection

God doesn't call you into every room, just the ones where your energy can multiply instead of evaporating.

6. The Domino Rule

Every kind act you do is a domino waiting to fall. You can't control when or where it'll fall, but when it does, it'll knock over ten others you didn't even know existed.

Your Quarterly Challenge

Send one message every few months that starts with "No reason for this message—just wanted to say hope you're doing well." You'll be shocked how many people respond with "You have no idea how much I needed this today." That's not random. That's *reach*.

7. For the Introverts

You don't need to work the room—you just need to make *one* person feel seen.

Your Game Plan

- Pre-research two or three people before every event.
- Ask them meaningful questions rather than just making small talk, like, "What's something you're currently curious about?"
- Follow up in writing. Your quiet thoughtfulness *is* your advantage.

Your Mantra

"I don't need to know everyone, I just to know someone well."

8. For the Extroverts

You already have the energy—now make it *memorable.*

Your Game Plan

- For every story you tell, ask one question back.
- Be the connector, not the spotlight.
- Leave people feeling lighter than they were when you found them.

Your Mantra

"My energy isn't just contagious, it's purposeful."

9. Gratitude Habit Tracker

Use this to build your new thank-you reflex:

WEEK	WHOM YOU THANKED	FORMAT	WHY IT MATTERED
Week 1		Handwritten	
Week 2		Text/DM	
Week 3		Verbal	
Week 4		Public shout-out	

At the end of the month, review:
- Which gestures felt the most natural?
- Which ones created unexpected returns?
- What did you learn about the *kind of energy* you bring into rooms?

10. The "Net + Work" Formula

Networking = Net (Reciprocity + Gratitude) × Work (Consistency + Faith)

It's not about forcing outcomes, it's about *staying in motion.* When you keep showing up, giving freely, and trusting that the right people will cross your path, your "network" becomes a safety net woven by grace. When you start wondering, *What if every person I met was a divine appointment, not for what they could give me but for what I was meant to give* them?, then you'll have a mindset that changes everything, because you'll stop chasing opportunities and start *attracting* them.

Keep your energy generous. Keep your posture grateful. Keep your reach within reach.

When Connection Turns into a Compass

Even though favor doesn't come with a GPS, doors will start to open. Paths will connect. People will appear at exactly the right time. For a while, it'll feel like the universe is your project manager. But then the map goes quiet and the calls slow down. The momentum stalls. And you start wondering, *Wait...did I lose it?*

But you didn't lose it. You just entered the part of the story where God trades *opportunity* for *orientation*. Because sometimes the same favor that once moved you forward has to pull you inward. He lets you get "lost" long enough to remember the difference between His plan and your platform.

That's the sacred tension between connection and calling: one expands you; the other refines you. You can only network your way so far before God says, "Now it's just Me and you again." And it's in that quiet recalibration, that uncomfortable stillness, where you rediscover not just your direction but your identity—your "why." You might think you're lost, but really, you're about to find yourself. Faith will become your only compass and you'll remember who you were before the world told you who to be.

CHAPTER 11

Lost and Found—The Truth About Purpose They Never Told You

Nobody warns you that success has an echo. After all the noise, all the meetings, all the "You're really doing it!" texts, there's a silence that feels louder than the applause ever did. It's that quiet space between *doing well* and *feeling whole*, where your calendar's full but your soul feels a little misplaced.

That's the paradox of momentum: it can carry you so far you forget who's driving. Sometimes, God lets the engine stall on purpose, not to punish you, but to park you long enough to ask, "Do you still recognize the person steering this thing?" Psychologists call it identity diffusion, the moment when your roles outgrow your roots. Faith calls it grace in disguise, the holy pause where God hides you to rebuild you. When the noise fades and the spotlight cools, your soul finally gets reintroduced to itself.

The Great Purpose Panic

The world has lied to you about purpose. Somewhere between your kindergarten teacher asking "What do you want to be when you grow up?" and your boss asking "Where do you see yourself in five years?", someone slipped in the word "purpose" and made it sound like you're supposed to *find* it, like it's hiding somewhere between a LinkedIn post and a TED Talk thumbnail. The internet has convinced us that our "why" is out there just waiting for each one of us, whispering through vision boards and latte art. Meanwhile, most of us are staring at our reflections in the microwave at 11 p.m. and wondering if our purpose is just to survive until Friday.

Here's the truth nobody has put on a mug: purpose isn't found, it's formed. If you've ever thought, *I should have my life figured out by now*, congratulations, you're human! And probably really tired. The disciples didn't have their lives figured out, either, when Jesus said, "Follow me." Faith always starts before clarity sets in. We don't get the map, we get the next step. That's why feeling lost isn't a failure of faith or focus. On the contrary—it's the birthplace of both.

A CFO friend of mine exemplified the tricky nature of finding purpose when he spent six months trying to "find himself" after leaving a job he hated. He meditated, journaled, and took every personality test he could find. (One told him he was "a golden retriever with anxiety." I tilted my head to the side and said, "Huh?") But after all that soul-searching, he still felt lost.

As he was telling me how lost he felt, I realized a core truth: being lost isn't the problem. The problem is assuming we *shouldn't* be lost. We panic when life doesn't have turn-by-turn directions, but that restlessness is actually neurological progress. Specifically, it's neuroplasticity, the process of our brain literally rewiring itself when we do something new or uncomfortable. When you're spiraling because life feels directionless, your brain's not broken! It's under renovation. God works the same way: He builds in silence. Think about Noah, who spent decades of hammering with no rain in sight. But the silence wasn't punishment, it was preparation.

"Find your purpose" is possibly the most successful marketing slogan in human history, and one of the most misleading. Like there's a cosmic Dropbox labeled *You_FinalVersion.pdf* sitting somewhere in the clouds, waiting for us to find it and download it. So, we go hunting. We read books, binge podcasts, and sign up for online courses led by people who use too many hand gestures and say "alignment" in every other sentence. The self-help industry has turned clarity into a subscription service, and the purpose industrial complex has been cashing in ever since.

But you can't buy clarity, you *build* it. Purpose grows roots every time you help someone else move toward theirs. The kind of meaning that appears when your focus shifts from "What do I want?" to "What can I give?" is self-transcendence. It's the same truth Jesus hinted at when

He said, "Whoever wants to save their life will lose it, but whoever loses their life for My sake will find it." So stop gripping so hard and start giving more, and know that when you feel like nothing's happening, actually, everything probably *is*.

That uneasy "in-between" feeling is Heaven's version of a construction zone. There's dust, there's noise, there are detours...but there's also design. I call it Holy Hard Hat season. That's when you have no clue what God's building, but you keep showing up anyway. You pray, you send the résumé, you try again. At its core, purpose is the relationships you have with others *and* with yourself. Purpose runs on serotonin—the quiet, steady neurotransmitter of belonging and peace.

The Lie of "Almost" and the Years of Being "Lost"

For years, I lived in the land of almosts. The job that almost worked. The project that almost took off. The relationship that almost made sense. "Almost" hurts because it flirts with fulfillment—you glimpse what could have been and mourn what never was. But Heaven uses almosts like rehearsal footage, because every disappointment fine-tunes your discernment and every delay strengthens your direction. In other words, it's prediction error learning—your brain updates its model every time reality doesn't match expectation. Every "no" is really just "not yet." Every detour is data. And sometimes the unanswered prayer is mercy wearing camouflage.

Closely related to almosts are the years that don't go according to plan, the ones that are supposed to be the glow-up but turn out to be more of a slow burn. I used to call those my "lost years." You know the ones: the job that paid well but drained you dry. The situationship that was almost love but mostly therapy. The side project that had "potential" (which is adult code for "This will never make money").

For the longest time, I treated those seasons like embarrassing footnotes, phases I hoped God had quietly deleted from my highlight reel. But now I realize lost doesn't mean wasted. Lost just means God was teaching me in a language I didn't understand yet. Faith and psychology agree on this more than either side probably realizes. Psychologists call it the progress principle: the measurable joy that comes from small, visible wins even when the big picture feels uncertain.

Faith calls it stewardship: showing up faithfully in the little things until you're trusted with bigger ones. Lost years aren't dead space, they're divine training grounds.

During those lost-but-not-really-lost years, I had what I now call Purpose Anxiety™—that buzzing, restless feeling that your résumé looks fine, but your soul's filing complaints nonetheless. You scroll past someone's engagement post and someone else's promotion, and suddenly you're wondering if you accidentally slept through your own destiny. And then the mental gymnastics start: *Maybe my purpose is hiding in Bali. Maybe I need another certification. Maybe I should take a nap.*

Researchers might call this cognitive dissonance—i.e., when your outer life doesn't match your inner story—but I call it a Tuesday. What's more important to remember, though, is that the tension you feel when your reality doesn't match your potential isn't failure, it's feedback. It's your spirit whispering, "We're not done yet."

I saw this happen to an intern I once had working for me. He lost it halfway through a mind-numbing spreadsheet—he slammed his pen down and sighed, saying, "This can't be my purpose." Then a year later, that same kid called me and said, "Hey, remember that spreadsheet I hated? It taught me analytics. I just used those skills to start a nonprofit."

Meaning is sneaky like that: it hides inside the mundane until hindsight puts a halo on it. Your "meaningless" job? Your "wasted" degree? Your "random" season? In truth, they're apprenticeships. Every task you resent today might become the skill that redeems you tomorrow.

I found myself in a similar where's-the-meaning? situation a few years ago when I applied for a dream job. I swore it was *the one.* I nailed every interview; I even bought new shoes. Then came the email: "We've decided to go in another direction."

Cool, Brian, I fumed. *Thanks for ruining my week and my self-esteem.* I spiraled hard, convinced I'd missed my one shot at greatness. But eventually I realized that *not* getting that job was the best thing that had ever happened to me, because if I would have taken that job, there would likely be no Reach With John and this book would certainly not exist. Sometimes, God closes doors for us to keep us from getting off track. Post-traumatic growth is how our brain and spirit get stronger through stress—every rejection builds emotional muscle for the weight we haven't lifted yet. God doesn't waste rejection, He recycles it into readiness.

But of course, when you're in the middle of the lost years, it doesn't feel noble. It feels like your life's buffering on dial-up. That's because your brain craves certainty more than progress. It would rather stay in a mediocre situation it understands than leap into an unknown one that might be better. Your nervous system does the same thing: it clings to the familiar even when the familiar is unhealthy.

The cure for both of these phenomena isn't a massive leap of faith, it's making micro-moves that prove motion is safe again. Send the email. Have the conversation. Apply for the role. Each small step tells your nervous system, "See? We didn't die." That's how courage grows: one nervous yes at a time. It can also happen one accidental yes at a time, like when I got stuck overnight in Denver after a canceled flight. Annoyed, I opened my laptop, logged onto airport Wi-Fi, and applied for a random conference talk slot out of pure boredom. That "random" decision became the start of my speaking career. Every detour, every reroute is grace in disguise.

That rerouting happened again years later as I was driving to a speaking gig. I was half-awake and running late when I took the wrong exit. Annoyed, I pulled into a random coffee shop to figure out directions. The owner struck up a conversation. He asked what I did, I told him about my talks, and he said, "We actually need a keynote for our company retreat next month. You free?"

That wrong exit became the right assignment. It was serendipity bias, when what felt like a mistake was just divine timing in street clothes. You can't miss what's meant for you—you can only arrive there unconventionally.

So, if you feel lost, congratulations! You're collecting data your future self will cash in on. Being lost isn't failure, it's field research. Confusion is proof that you're still curious. Restlessness means there's more to uncover. Every "lost" season is both science and scripture in motion. It's pattern integration—your brain is connecting dots that didn't make sense before—and it's revelation. God is showing you how every thread was intentional. You weren't abandoned, you were being rerouted. GPS never says "lost"—it just keeps repeating "Recalculating."

Pivot Moments

Every meaningful life has a moment when the soundtrack changes. It's rarely loud. It's rarely dramatic. It usually happens when you least expect it. For my friend Jordan, that moment came on a Tuesday night (of course) in a fluorescent-lit office that smelled like burnt coffee and panic. Jordan was one of those golden-résumé people: honor-roll everything, top internships, could power a small city on ambition alone. Every mentor, professor, and career quiz agreed: leadership was her calling. So she sprinted straight into it, landing a management job right out of college. The title looked great on paper. The paycheck looked even better.

Six months later, she was drowning. Her calendar looked like a losing game of Tetris. Her anxiety had its own parking spot. Every morning, she woke up wondering why the "dream" felt like drywall dust in her lungs. But quitting would have felt like betrayal, not of the job but of the identity she'd built around it.

One late night at the office, as she was doomscrolling through spreadsheets, she heard quiet sniffles from the intern's cubicle. The kid had messed up a client presentation and was on the verge of tears. Jordan could've kept typing, but she didn't. Instead, she pulled up a chair next to the intern. For the next hour, they rewrote slides, practiced delivery, and talked about fear and failure until the intern finally exhaled.

The next morning, the intern nailed it: no stumbles, no panic, just quiet confidence. And Jordan, exhausted and dangerously close to burnout, felt something she hadn't felt in months: peace. Not adrenaline. Not excitement. Peace. That was when she realized that her purpose wasn't to lead, it was to lift. Not to command people, but to develop them.

That changed everything, although she didn't quit her job. She *did* redefine it, though—she stopped chasing outcomes and started investing in people. And something holy happened: her team started thriving. Productivity rose. Turnover dropped. And joy, real joy, crept back into the room. She had achieved cognitive realignment, which happens when your internal definition of success finally syncs with your emotional truth. Faith calls it surrender, the moment you stop forcing outcomes and start following alignment.

I had a pivot moment, too. Early in my career, I thought purpose was performance: titles, applause, the next rung on the ladder. I collected achievements the way kids collect Pokémon cards because that's what I thought worth looked like. Then one day I got invited to give a talk at a community college. It involved twenty students, bad lighting, and a microphone that smelled suspiciously like coffee breath. Not exactly the TED Talk stage I'd dreamed of.

But afterward, a student came up and said, "Hey, I didn't think people like you ever felt lost. It's kind of nice to know I'm not broken." That line stopped me cold. In that moment, I realized my purpose wasn't to *impress* people, it was to *connect* with them. And that was going to come from making a deeper impact, not being on a bigger stage. I pivoted from performing purpose to *practicing* it, from seeking spotlight to stewarding stories. Purpose isn't about doing more. It's about doing what matters most, faithfully.

My pivot moment was a positive one, but often, the hardest part about realigning your life is that it usually starts with something falling apart. You don't pivot in comfort, you pivot in chaos, and that can feel like failure. But it isn't! When you outgrow an old purpose, it means you've evolved. Viewed through that lens, every experience becomes raw material for redemption.

Here's where science and Spirit overlap beautifully. Our brains crave coherence, the sense that life makes narrative sense. When a new insight finally "clicks," the prefrontal cortex lights up like Times Square. That neurological reward is what psychologists call insight-based learning. Spiritually, we just call it revelation. Either way, it's the aha moment when you finally understand why the delay happened, why the door closed, or why the heartbreak hurt so bad. In other words, it's your brain and your faith shaking hands.

Every revelation rewires you for trust; every pivot is proof that grace still works. You could've stayed bitter, but you didn't. You could've doubled down on control, but you didn't. Instead, you listened. You turned. And when you pivot with God, even pain becomes productive—your purpose doesn't vanish, it changes uniforms. The teacher becomes the mentor. The performer becomes the encourager. The leader becomes the servant.

We treat lost like it's a four-letter word: "I'm lost." "Oh no, let's fix that immediately!" But maybe lost isn't broken, maybe it's just being free. When you're lost, nobody expects you to have all the answers. You get to explore again. You get to breathe again. You get to eat cereal for dinner and call it "mindful carb therapy."

Being lost means you're *not* on autopilot. You're awake and paying attention, and you've stepped off the predictable path long enough for God to surprise you. Abraham didn't know where he was going when he left home, he just knew Who he was following. Faith doesn't hand you a map, it hands you a compass that points to presence.

Mind you, a few years back, I got literally lost during a hike in Arizona. I thought I was following the trail, but it turned out I was following a guy named Gary who just *looked* confident. Two hours later, I had no signal, one granola bar, and the kind of sweat that makes you question your life choices. Somewhere between panic and prayer, I stopped to catch my breath...and saw the sky.

It was ridiculous: a sherbet-colored sunset painted across the mountains. The kind of beauty you only notice when you stop trying to beat daylight. That moment rewired me. I realized maybe God sometimes lets the signal drop so you'll finally look up. You can't see the horizon when you're staring at the map.

Neuroscientists say that the default-mode network—that's the brain circuit that sparks creativity—lights up most when we're daydreaming, wandering, or...lost. That's why your best ideas show up in the shower or mid-drive with no destination—your brain finally has room to breathe. Faith calls that being still and knowing. Science calls it pattern recognition. Either way, it's the same miracle: stillness reveals strategy. So, if you feel lost right now, just know that your neurons and your soul are collaborating on a new blueprint.

WITHIN REACH TOOLKIT
How to Escape from the Purpose Loop

Even though we love to talk about "finding" purpose, the people who say they've found it aren't really done, because purpose grows as we do. Social media has complicated the equation by making purpose competitive—now everyone's "on a mission to revolutionize human consciousness through synergistic leadership" even if really, they're just selling staplers. We've branded purpose into performance art, but real purpose doesn't need PR—it needs persistence.

The people who are *actually* changing the world rarely post about it because they're too busy living it. The teacher who stays late to help the kid everyone else gave up on. The janitor who cracks jokes during layoffs to keep morale alive. The mom who still leaves Post-its that say "You got this!" in a lunchbox she can barely afford. *That's* purpose. Quiet. Unpaid. Relentless.

But the goal isn't to *find* your purpose, it's to stay findable *by* it, so keep moving, keep serving, and keep paying attention. If you want real freedom, stop demanding the map and start trusting the Maker instead. Follow your purpose one faithful step at a time. Move. Try. Fail. Pray. Repeat. Laugh in between. When you finally stop needing every detail, you make room for divine detail, the kind that only appears in motion. You'll look back one day and realize the detours *were* the design.

The Purpose Loop, or How to Stop Chasing Clarity and Start Building It

PHASE	WHAT IT FEELS LIKE	WHAT'S ACTUALLY HAPPENING	WHAT TO DO
Lost	"Nothing's working." Confusion. Comparison.	Your brain is rewiring (neuroplasticity). God is reordering your steps.	Stop diagnosing and start observing. Ask, "What might this be teaching me?"
Learning	"Why does everything feel hard?"	Growth hormones and neural circuits are under construction.	Replace panic with practice. Pick one small, uncomfortable action per day.
Aligned	"This finally feels like peace."	Dopamine drops, serotonin rises. You've built endurance, not excitement.	Guard your rhythms. Peace is proof of progress.
Led	"I don't know exactly where this is going, but I trust it."	Faith and pattern recognition merge.	Keep serving. Keep showing up. Keep laughing through the unknown.

Remember, you don't "find" your purpose, you *recognize* it mid-motion.

Faith Prompts for When You Feel Lost

First, think about the neural gospel:

- **Neuroplasticity = sanctification.** Your brain changes through repetition. So does your character. Every time you choose grace over fear, you're literally rewriting your neural wiring.
- **The Zeigarnik Effect = unfinished faith.** Your mind might hate incomplete stories, but God loves them. Trust is the muscle built during those unfinished paragraphs.
- **Dopamine vs. serotonin.** Dopamine is the spark (passion). Serotonin is the peace (purpose). You need both, just not in equal doses.
- **Pattern recognition = revelation.** The reason you "see it now" in hindsight is that both your brain *and* God work in patterns. They connect the dots when you're ready, not when you're impatient.

While keeping those principles in mind:

1. Pray this: "God, I don't need to know where this is going. I just need to know You're still in it."
2. Ask this:

   - What part of me is God trying to grow while I wait?
   - Am I chasing clarity or cultivating character?
   - What if this delay isn't punishment but protection?

3. Write this:

   - List three "almost" moments from your past.
   - Next to each, jot down what you learned, who you met, or what skill appeared later because of that "almost."
   - Connect the dots. You'll see divine choreography hiding in what you once called coincidence.

Practical Exercises

1. The purpose inventory.

Draw a line down the middle of a page. On one side, list the things that *energize* you (dopamine). On the other, list what *grounds* you (serotonin). Your purpose is usually where those two intersect in service of others.

2. The 1% rule.

Do something today that moves you forward by 1%. Not 10%. Not 100%. Just evidence that you're still in motion. God doesn't need massive leaps— He honors micro-moves.

3. The spiritual GPS check.

At the end of each week, ask:

- Did I feel peace in what I did?
- Did I love people well?
- Did I try to control outcomes that weren't mine?

The more you can answer yes to the first two and no to the last, the closer you're driving to purpose.

4. Reflect in your journal.

Ask:

- When was the last time I felt truly *alive*—not just busy, but present?
- What was I doing, who was I with, and what values was I living out in that moment?

That's your breadcrumb trail. Follow it.

5. Mantra for the week.

"I'm not lost. I'm being led. Peace is not the proof that everything's done, it's the sign that I'm finally in alignment."

Every lost season is a holy classroom. Every unanswered prayer is an invitation to build trust. Every reroute is Heaven's way of saying, "We're still on time." So, keep walking, keep laughing, keep serving. You don't need the whole map when you know the Maker.

What You Find in the Quiet

The thing about being lost is that you start listening differently—when the noise fades, the signal gets clearer. You start noticing God in details you used to scroll past, in traffic lights that hold you just long enough to breathe, in songs that somehow play the line you needed most, in people who remind you that you're still becoming. That's the gift of being found: you stop chasing validation and start valuing direction. You realize you don't need every answer, just the faith to take the next step. And maybe most importantly, you start seeing the people who helped build you, the ones whose fingerprints are quietly all over your story. Purpose is shaped in relationships—with the mentors, the family, the icons, the unexpected voices who taught you how to keep digging when life got heavy.

For me, I received invaluable lessons from two unlikely teachers: one with a movie career and one with a toolbox. One taught me about chasing greatness; the other taught me about finding gold in ordinary things. Sometimes, you realize the treasure you've been chasing was sitting next to you the whole time.

CHAPTER 12

Lessons from Legends and The Search For My Own Gold

It's strange how the loudest lessons in your life sometimes come from people who never meant to teach them. For me, it was a Hollywood star and a man who fixed things for a living. Both taught me something about greatness...and both did it without realizing they were preaching.

It started the way most revelations in my life have started: in the middle of an ordinary day. One part Netflix binge, one part nostalgia spiral, and one unexpected gut punch from God that felt suspiciously like a Will Smith monologue. That's how divine curriculum works—you don't get a syllabus, just sudden clarity between scenes. Right there, watching a man on screen chase validation and thinking about my dad in the garage chasing integrity, I realized something that hit harder than any movie ending: *We're all searching for gold, we just define it differently.*

The Purgatory Between "Someday..." and "Go!"

There's an awkward waiting room between "I'll do it someday" and "I'm doing it right now." I call it dream-chasing purgatory—it's the hazy middle ground where your dreams feel too big for your zip code and God seems to be on silent mode. Like when I was living in Toledo, Ohio. Not exactly where dreams go to thrive. More like where they sit on the couch and say, "I'll get up in five minutes." I kept waiting for a sign. A lightning bolt; maybe a prophetic billboard that said, "Move to California, John." Instead, I got lake-effect snow and Arby's coupons.

But then one afternoon, Will Smith (yes, *that* Will Smith, the Fresh

Prince of Timely Advice) was doing an interview, and I half-heard him say: "Anyone who's considering making a huge move in their life needs to read this book." I almost ignored it. Then he said, "This book will change your life." And suddenly I was locked in like a toddler who just heard the Coco melon intro with 2% battery left. That's DEFCON 1 attention right there.

The book? *The Alchemist* by Paulo Coelho. It's about a boy named Santiago who dreams of finding treasure made of gold. Along the way, he meets an alchemist who teaches him the truth: the real transformation isn't turning metal into gold, it's turning fear into faith. That plotline hit me hard, because to be honest, my faith back then was more like a subscription trial—active, but definitely expiring soon.

I got the book. I was only a few pages in when something shifted. Honestly, the book should've been titled *John, Stop Talking and Read This Before You Do Something Dumb,* because the moment I opened it, something clicked. Suddenly, Toledo Purgatory had an exit ramp, and I was flooring it west. It wasn't just Will Smith's voice or Coelho's wisdom, it was like God whispering, "You've been asking for a sign. Here's one in paperback."

In that moment, I stopped waiting for "someday" and started planning my (literal) next move with a different kind of GPS: a God Positioning System.

My Dad: The Original Alchemist

Growing up, my dad and I had what therapists would gently label "creative tension." He thought fun was a federal offense. I thought discipline was a rumor spread by people who hated joy. But beneath all that friction, something was happening, though I definitely didn't see it then. Every chore, every curfew, every "Stop being dramatic, John!" was actually his version of faith formation disguised as fatherhood. Still, it took me years to realize that my dad was my first alchemist. Mr. Miyagi was the second one. Instead of teaching me karate, Dad's version of "Wax on, wax off" involved mowing lawns and learning to use a wrench correctly.

By the time I was ready to leave for California, our relationship had evolved. He wasn't just my dad anymore, he was the man quietly teaching me that ordinary effort becomes extraordinary faith when you keep showing up.

Fast-forward to August 2005. I was standing in the same cracked driveway where I'd first learned to ride a bike. My car smelled like French fries and freedom. Dad walked up, eyes glassy, heart heavy, and handed me an envelope. I thought, *Finally!* The parental downpayment on my dreams. Maybe a few twenties. Maybe a check. Maybe a "Get out of broke free" card.

I opened it. No money. Just a letter. But the first line stopped me cold and gave me insta-chills: "There's gold in them hills in California."

I froze. It didn't feel like *just* my dad speaking, it felt like God borrowing his handwriting. Like the same Father who'd been teaching me patience through one dad was now sending me courage through another. The parallels between his letter and *The Alchemist* were chilling. So, I packed the letter, the book, and all the ambition I could fit into a beat-up car that needed more prayer than gas. Then I waved goodbye to my hero and headed westward.

The Road West (Co-Starring Mom)

If this were a movie, you'd cue the solo montage as our hero headed west on his quest for gold. I can see it plain as day as I type those words. And my journey *was* just like that, except for one minor difference: our hero was going with his mommy...

When I told Mom I was driving to California, she didn't even blink. She said, "Okay, but how are you getting there?"

"I'm driving," I said confidently.

She stared. "Over my dead body. When do we leave?"

So yeah, Mom was coming. The first few hours were cinematic: windows down, dreams up, the Midwest fading behind us like a bad haircut. We sang, joked, and shared snacks that should've been illegal in at least 17 states. But around Hour Six, something changed. The scenery went quiet. My confidence got quiet. Billboards started speaking to me: "Adopt a dog." Cool. "Try beef jerky." Also cool. "Don't panic." ...Okay, now I was panicking.

Somewhere between gas stations and self-doubt, Mom reached over, grabbed my hand, and said, "You're really doing it, huh?"

I nodded, pretending to be brave.

She smiled. "Good. You *should* be scared. It means it matters."

I swear I could feel God in the passenger seat, too, probably rolling His eyes and saying something like, "Finally! You're driving in the direction I've been hinting at since Chapter One."

We made pit stops, prayed over bad coffee, and laughed at the absurdity of chasing a dream 3,000 miles away with no plan and a car that made new noises daily. And somewhere on that highway, I realized, *Maybe God doesn't calm every storm. Maybe sometimes He just hops in and says, "Scoot over—I'll navigate."*

When we finally crossed into California, I swear the air actually smelled different, namely like hope, possibility, and car exhaust.

Mom looked at me with a proud but terrified face and asked, "So... What now?"

I laughed. "No idea."

That night, in a cheap motel with flickering neon lights and Wi-Fi that only worked if you prayed hard enough, we ate drive-through burgers in the parking lot. I pulled out Dad's letter again: "There's gold in them hills in California."

Mom smiled softly. "Your dad always knew you'd go find it."

And under that buzzing light, I finally got it: the gold wasn't fame. It wasn't money. It wasn't success. It was courage. It was love. It was obedience, the kind that doesn't wait for perfect timing, just God's nudge. Because sometimes faith looks less like a miracle and more like motion. You don't walk on water unless you *step out of the boat.*

That night, I prayed the most honest prayer I'd ever prayed: "God, I don't know what I'm doing. But I'll keep going if You keep showing up." And I swear I heard Him whisper back, "Deal. Just keep going."

Not stopping is huge, because every time we take a step toward something that matters, our brain releases dopamine. It's our body's way of saying, "Look at you, brave little miracle!" That dopamine rush also reflects what psychologists call the progress principle, and it happens because our brains crave movement, not necessarily completion.

Faith and fear feel so close because they're both responses to something you can't see yet. One paralyzes you; the other propels you. But you don't need the whole plan—you just need to prove to your brain (and maybe your Creator) that you're willing to take the next step. Motion creates meaning. Fear doesn't mean you should stop! It just means Heaven's trying to get your attention.

WITHIN REACH TOOLKIT
Find Your Gold Map™

STEP	CONCEPT	PSYCHOLOGICAL WHY	FAITH FRAME	ACTION STEP
1. Define your Santiago moment.	Identify the dream that won't leave you alone.	Naming intention activates the goal-pursuit network in your prefrontal cortex; focus follows clarity.	God doesn't give you random dreams. Those are divine breadcrumbs!	Write it down, even if it feels ridiculous. Heaven honors bold ink.
2. Name your alchemist.	Recognize who or what awakened your belief.	Gratitude boosts serotonin and builds cognitive resilience.	Every "mentor" is a messenger.	Text or call that person today. Tell them what they sparked.
3. Identify your Mom moment.	Know your emotional anchor: the person, quote, or faith that steadies you.	The secure base theory says that feeling stable increases risk tolerance.	God uses people to hold us steady when fear shakes the wheel.	Keep a note, verse, or photo nearby for the days your faith forgets.
4. Keep your letter visible.	A daily cue reignites motivation circuits.	Visual reminders activate associative memory, making your "why" stay top of mind.	Faith needs a focal point.	Write your own version of "There's gold in them hills." Post it somewhere sacred.
5. Move anyway.	Action >anxiety.	Movement releases endorphins that lower the fear response.	God can't steer a parked car.	Take the next small, brave step, even if your voice shakes.

You don't find your gold by waiting, you find it by *trusting* and then moving. Because gold isn't out there buried under them hills—it's created inside you every time you move forward in faith, laugh through the fear, and let God ride shotgun. So, pack your courage, your favorite people, and maybe a few drive-through tacos. Your own hills are waiting. And trust me, they're *holy ground*.

Redefining What It Means to Be Rich

The older I get, the more I realize the richest people I know don't lead with their résumés. They lead with who they've loved well. They're the ones who somehow always have time to call, who remember your kid's name, who show up when everyone else just sends a "thinking of you" text.

That's the paradox of the search for gold: you can chase shininess for a lifetime and still feel empty, or you can invest in people and realize you've been sitting on compound interest the whole time. My dad was someone who never measured success in square footage or salary bands—he measured it in presence, in whether you left people better than you found them. Maybe *that's* the real wealth transfer I inherited: not assets, but atmosphere. Because one day the applause fades, the job titles reset, and the trophies start collecting dust. But relationships keep paying dividends long after the market closes.

In the sacred math of connection, empathy accrues, kindness compounds, and the only ROI that matters is how much love you left in circulation. We're about to dig into relationship ROI and the currency of calling, but first, here's a teaser: what you *give away* is what makes you rich.

CHAPTER 13

Relationship ROI: The Math They Don't Teach You in School

We talk about investing like it's only about money—stocks, savings, and real estate are the usual suspects. But no one tells you the highest-yield investment on earth is a text that starts with "Hey, just thinking about you."

It's wild how the market of human connection works. You can spend years hustling for influence, and then one act of genuine kindness buys you more credibility than any business card ever could. That kind of social capital consists of the trust, loyalty, and goodwill that compound quietly in the background of your life. I call it that the gospel of reciprocity. It's the divine reminder that giving isn't loss, it's leverage.

The return on relationships is measured in the peace that comes from knowing you've poured into people who'd still show up even if you lost everything. When life audits you—and it will!—the question won't be "What did you earn?" but rather "Who did you build?" Which is why Relationship ROI is so important. This is the chapter where we run the numbers on love and find out that the only account worth growing is the one that can't be spent.

Reciprocity Is Your Secret Weapon

It started with a group chat. And not just any group chat—it was the kind you name something overconfident like *The Wolf Pack* even though none of us had been within 200 feet of a wolf, a gym, or a consistent social life since graduation.

Fueled by caffeine and misplaced optimism, I typed, "Hey fellas, we should all catch up soon. Been too long."

Delivered. Read by three. No response.

Ah, yes, the modern equivalent of being ghosted by people who literally share your last name in a fantasy football league. I stared at the screen longer than I care to admit. I tried to justify it. *Maybe they're busy*, I thought. *Maybe they're typing. Maybe they died.*

Nope. Alive. Just emotionally unavailable.

The realization hit me like a late Venmo request: relationships depreciate faster than a new car leaving the lot if you don't maintain them. The truly scary part is that no one ever taught us *how* to maintain them. We learned that the mitochondria was the powerhouse of the cell but not that "checking in" is the powerhouse of human connection. We studied supply and demand, but never empathy and reciprocity. We got an A for memorizing the periodic table but zero credit for helping a friend through a panic attack before a presentation. As a result, now we find ourselves fluent in metrics but illiterate in meaning. Which is why we're about to get into the syllabus of Relationship ROI.

Relationships Are the New Currency

There's a hidden economy running under everything you do, and it's not dollars. It's *trust.* Every person you meet keeps a subconscious ledger. They might not know it consciously, but their heart does: who makes deposits (effort, empathy, curiosity) and who makes withdrawals (neglect, ego, ghosting)? That invisible math decides how people feel when your name lights up their phone.

You don't pay mentors with money, not at first. You pay with energy. With curiosity. With follow-through. You pay with that small-yet-powerful text: "Hey, I applied that advice you gave me and it worked." *That's* a deposit.

Similarly, you build friendships through micro-moments: the "thinking of you" message, the "I saw this and thought of you" meme, the random call on a random Tuesday that conveys "You still matter to me." Those small actions are the emotional equivalent of compound interest. The catch? No one tells you about this hidden economy until you've already overdrafted your emotional account.

When I first moved to California, I was broke enough that "mentorship" sounded like a subscription I couldn't afford. So, I started cold-messaging professionals on LinkedIn, offering to buy coffee I couldn't actually pay for. One person replied: "Keep your $5. Just come with good questions." That one conversation turned into three, which turned into a job lead, which turned into a career pivot.

All from a zero investment in dollars but with a full investment in curiosity and gratitude. That's the first truth about Relationship ROI: the richest people in the world are those who never stop investing in others, because connection is the only currency that compounds faster than time. Still, most of us are bad at this because no one taught us *how* to be good at it. Our default model for relationships is basically every college group project ever: one person doing all the work while everyone else coasts on vibes.

We overinvest in people who give us nothing back ("I can fix them" energy). We underinvest in the ones who always show up ("Sorry, bro, been busy" energy). We assume that effort equals outcome...until life reminds us that people aren't spreadsheets. But we don't do this because we're terrible people, this happens because our *brains* are lazy.

Neuroscience proves it: the prefrontal cortex, our logic manager, prunes unused connections over time. That means when we haven't reached out to someone in months, our brain starts dulling the emotional connection we had with them. We don't feel distant because we stopped caring, we stopped caring *because* our brain decided that person isn't "active data" anymore. In other words, our neurons are doing the ghosting.

But there's good news! The brain is plastic and it can rewire itself. Every time you push through the awkward "Should I text them?" moment, you retrain your neural circuitry to value connection again. That tiny reach-out is spiritual strength disguised as social effort.

I learned this truth the hard way. I had a coworker who was basically family—we shared inside jokes, lunch breaks, and mutual trauma from endless meetings that could've been emails. Then came promotions, moves, new jobs, life. I drafted a text three times: "Hey, man, been a while. How are you?" But then I deleted it every time. "Too much time has passed," I told myself. "It'll be weird now."

Two months later, I found out he'd moved across the country. No goodbye, no closure, just gone. That moment taught me a hard lesson:

the longer you wait, the heavier the phone gets. And silence has interest rates, too.

The Hidden Science of Emotional ROI

Humans are emotional accountants—we keep score even when we swear we don't. We notice who texts first, who remembers birthdays, who claps loudly online but stays quiet in real life. We build emotional balance sheets, and when the math doesn't add up, we call it burnout or disappointment.

Behavioral economics calls this reciprocity imbalance. When we give expecting an equal return, our brain's reward system rewires around resentment instead of joy. That's why love feels exhausting when it's conditional. That's also why *real* generosity—the kind that expects nothing back—feels like freedom.

The fix? Stop chasing symmetry and start valuing consistency. Don't count one-off gestures, count patterns. Relationships are about rhythm: a flow of giving, resting, receiving, and repeating. And remember that the brain's reward system is wired for reciprocity.

Give kindness. → Dopamine.
Receive it back. → Serotonin.

It's neuroscience's way of saying, "Keep doing that! It keeps you alive." This is why genuine connection feels like oxygen: it regulates your nervous system, reduces cortisol, and boosts immunity. Translation: good friends literally make you harder to kill.

If you've ever said, "I'm just not a people person," that's not personality, that's unpracticed biology. We were designed for dependence. Not *co*dependence, but divine *inter*dependence, the "iron sharpens iron" kind. Even Jesus built a team before He built a ministry. He could've done the whole thing solo—water-walking, healing, motivational speaking—but He chose *twelve dudes with mixed résumés and questionable time management skills.* God could've stayed theoretical. Instead, He showed up incarnate, a walking reminder that love only works when it shows up *in person.*

The Real Formula Behind Every Door That's Ever Opened

I once worked with a manager who treated human connections like tax deductions: nice if convenient, but never the priority. He'd start every Monday meeting with "Let's jump right in," skipping the small talk as if it were beneath him. So one day, just for fun (and science), I decided to test the ROI of empathy. Before the meeting, I asked, "How was your weekend?"

He blinked, thrown off, then said, "Fine."

Next week I asked again and followed up about his son's baseball game he'd mentioned. His face softened. The next week, he asked *me* first. By Month Three, he was staying after meetings to talk about mentorship and purpose. The same man who had once seen people as data points started seeing them as divine appointments. The ROI? Trust skyrocketed. Communication improved. And the team who had once worked *for* him started working *with* him.

That's the thing about deposits: they rarely pay out instantly. Instead, they grow quietly in the background until the moment you need them most. I call that delayed compounding. Every text, every "thinking of you," every prayer you whisper for someone who'll never know it—none of that is wasted. They all accrue interest in unseen accounts. Then one day, you hit a wall, and a door opens you didn't even know existed. That's not luck, that's God paying dividends in divine timing.

The Faith Thread: God's Reciprocity Algorithm

If you strip the Bible down to one repeating equation, it's this: what you sow, you grow. Not instantly. Not always in the same soil. But inevitably, it'll grow. It's the spiritual version of compounding interest; it's grace multiplied by consistency.

Jesus never said, "Love people when they deserve it." He said, "Love your neighbor." Period. Love isn't a transaction, it's transformation in motion. When you pour into others, you don't just fill them, you expand your own emotional capacity to receive.

Psychology agrees—neuroscientists call this phenomenon the self-expansion theory. It's the idea that helping others broadens your identity and strengthens your sense of meaning. When you pour out, your brain literally expands its definition of *you*. It's God and gray matter high-fiving. That's why the people who seem most fulfilled aren't the ones chasing attention, they're the ones building bridges.

All that said, let's be honest: sometimes serving people feels one-sided. You give and give, and they vanish; you show up, and they forget; you invest, and it feels like a sunk cost. But what if that's the point? What if God uses those imbalanced equations to refine your motive? To teach you that serving others isn't about the applause, it's about the alignment?

The truth is simple: when your "why" is transactional, burnout is inevitable. But when your "why" is eternal, peace is nonnegotiable. *That's* the secret of purpose-led connection! It runs on grace, not guarantees.

The Leadership Trust Dividend

One of the weirdest lessons adulthood teaches you is that career success doesn't belong to the smartest person in the room, it belongs to the most *trusted*. The people who rise don't always have perfect résumés, but they do create emotional safety—they make meetings feel like conversations instead of court depositions. In corporate terms, that's called psycho-logical safety. In the kingdom of God, it's called *peace*. Same principle, different vocabulary.

When people trust you, they stop spending energy on self-defense and start spending it on creativity. Their nervous systems calm down and their prefrontal cortex opens up. You literally become a walking productivity hack, a human permission slip to exhale. That's why Scripture says, "Perfect love casts out fear." Turns out, perfect leadership does, too.

I saw this in action with a mentor I had once. He never raised his voice, but somehow, you always wanted to do better around him out of sheer respect. He didn't demand excellence, he inspired it. One day I asked him, "What's your secret?"

He smiled and said, "Trust is a credit line. You build it long before you need it." That hit me like divine algebra.

Every favor, every check-in, every moment of consistency is a deposit into that line of credit. That way, when crisis hits, you don't have to beg for buy-in, because you've already earned it. The people who trust you will extend grace you didn't even know was available. That's the Leadership Trust Dividend, and it's the miracle of compounding reliability. (It's also the magic of mirror neurons—your calm creates calm in others.)

When the Market Crashes but God Builds Bridges

But what happens when the account runs dry? When you've overdrawn your relational balance not out of malice but just out of neglect? That's the uncomfortable truth: withdrawals hit harder than deposits help. It's called loss aversion—our brains feel the sting of loss twice as intensely as the joy of gain.

One missed call. One "We should catch up soon" text that never leaves the launchpad. One too many "I'll reply later" responses. Before you know it, the line goes quiet and the friendship dissolves into static. This kind of emotional entropy is the slow unraveling of connection through inattention. But! Redemption is still available in the form of redemption repair attempts. God calls those *grace.*

I've been there—I remember a time when I ghosted a collaborator. Not intentionally; I was just drowning in deadlines and pretend-multitasking was a spiritual gift. Weeks turned into months and guilt turned into avoidance. Finally, I sent the text: "Hey, I dropped the ball. Not because you weren't important, but because I wasn't managing my time or my heart well. I'm sorry."

He replied, "Honestly, I respect you more for saying that."

That was when I came up with this formula:

The Apology Intserest Rate = Humility Compounds Faster Than Hustle

One honest confession can restore a relationship faster than 100 perfect performances can, because luckily, grace has a higher yield than pride does. Attention is resurrection power in disguise. A single "Hey, I was thinking about you" can revive a friendship that's been flatlined for years.

The enemy of connection isn't conflict, it's apathy, and the cure is consistent, small, faithful, follow-through. Its little deposits of presence—no grand gestures needed. You don't need to say everything, you just need to *show up.*

Personally, every door I've ever walked through had fingerprints on the handle. A friend who vouched. A mentor who believed. A stranger who said, "You seem like someone who could help." If I were to trace every major pivot in my life backward, I know I would see that it always leads to one thing: a person God placed there at the right time.

It's wild how Heaven writes stories using human hands. You think you're just having coffee, but God thinks you're building a bridge. The opportunity wasn't random and the timing wasn't coincidence. Divine connections always feel accidental on the surface, but in hindsight, they're orchestral. Every "random" encounter, every "wrong place, right time" moment? That's God running His own ROI equation: Relationship. Obedience. Impact.

The Reunion Effect

A few years after the ghost town group chat incident, I ran into half of those same guys at a wedding. Dim lights, bad DJ, open bar – the holy trinity of reconciliation. We locked eyes. No words at first, just that slow grin that said, "Wow... We made it."

And then, it happened: the laughter. Instant, effortless, like no time had passed. Inside jokes were resurrected. Old memories resurfaced. Years melted into minutes. That's the Reunion Effect, when dormant connections reactivate because the foundations were real. Your brain floods with oxytocin, your heart compresses time, and suddenly, you remember why that friendship mattered in the first place. The Reunion Effect is proof that love doesn't expire, it just waits for an update.

That, right there, is grace in motion. Every unanswered text, every awkward reconnection, every "Hey, I know it's been a while..." message—those are all acts of faith disguised as outreach. When you reach out, you're rebuilding trust *and* you're partnering with Heaven's restoration plan. You're saying, "I still believe this connection can live again." And God loves that posture, because that's what He does every day with us.

The Final Math

Here's the Relationship ROI math they don't teach you in school: Intentions are emotional Monopoly money. You can't deposit good vibes. Only follow-through counts.

- **Frequency beats intensity.** A steady trickle of care outperforms occasional fireworks.
- **Repair outruns perfection.** People trust vulnerability more than flawlessness.
- **Reciprocity has lag time.** The return rarely comes on your timeline, it comes on your *character's* timeline.
- **Relationships are the compound interest of life.** The earlier and more consistently you invest, the richer you become.

That last one is the most important. So, text the friend. Thank the mentor. Compliment the coworker. Forgive the one who stopped showing up—they might just be fighting battles you can't see.

Stop treating connection like extra credit. It's the curriculum! I guarantee that every open door in your life has someone's fingerprints on it. I also guarantee that every person who trusted you was a divine investment.

You can't always calculate the return, but I promise, the ROI of love always beats the market. In God's economy, nothing relational is ever wasted—not a word, not a coffee, not a kindness, not a single, awkward "Hey, it's been a while." Connection releases the same hormone—oxytocin—as prayer and worship do.

WITHIN REACH TOOLKIT
Relationship ROI

The connection formula is a simple one: **ROI = (Deposits × Time) ÷ Withdrawals**

Or in human terms, consistency beats charisma every time.

VARIABLE	DEFINITION	REAL-LIFE EXAMPLE	PAYOFF
D (Deposits)	Small acts of effort, empathy, and presence	"Hey, saw this and thought of you."	Builds trust and belonging
W (Withdrawals)	Neglect, ego, unkept promises	Ghosting. Forgetting birthdays. Silence.	Creates emotional debt
T (Time)	The space where faith + follow-through meet	Showing up consistently, not perfectly.	Turns effort into endurance
ROI (Return on Intentionality)	The peace, purpose, and opportunity born from faithful connection	Seeds you plant in others that bloom later.	Compound impact

Faith Prompts: Connection as Calling

1. Pray this: "God, teach me to see people as You see them— not as transactions, but as trust funds."
2. Ask this:
   - Who's been quietly faithful in my life whom I've failed to thank?
   - Who needs a second chance instead of another critique?
   - Where have I overinvested out of fear instead of love?

3. Write this: Create a Relational Balance Sheet with three columns:
   - Deposits I've made lately
   - Withdrawals I need to repair

- People I owe appreciation to

Then text one person from each column within 24 hours.

Exercises for Connection Growth

1. The five-minute rule.

Once a week, spend five minutes sending appreciation or encouragement—no agenda, no ask.

Science: Releases serotonin and strengthens your sense of purpose.
Faith: Turns gratitude into worship through action.

2. The bridge builder.

List one person you've "lost touch" with, then reach out with humility: "Hey, I was thinking about you. No reason other than gratitude." That one sentence could resurrect a friendship God still intends to use.

3. The follow-through audit.

Go through your texts, DMs, or emails. Circle every "Let's grab coffee soon." Pick *one* this week and actually do it. It's not scheduling, it's stewardship.

Journal Reflection

As you're journaling, remember that loss aversion means we feel losses twice as deeply as wins. That's why one "I'm sorry" can heal more than ten "I love you's." And when you offer grace, it compounds—every act of kindness reinforces neural pathways of safety and reminds your spirit that it's safe to love again.

Journal on this: "Which relationships in my life are running on old deposits? How can I start making new ones, not out of guilt, but gratitude?"

Reflect on how each person you're grateful for is connected to a moment of grace in your story. There's always a pattern, and the pattern always leads back to God's timing.

Mantras for the Week

"Small deposits. Steady returns."
"God's math doesn't subtract people, it multiplies peace."
"Relationships don't expire, they evolve."

Reframing the "R" in ROI

Every interaction is a seed and none of them are ever wasted. The text you send, the apology you offer, the thank-you you finally say—they don't just rebuild connection, they rebuild *character*. Because in God's economy, every relational act is spiritual investing. So, keep sowing. Keep showing up. Keep nurturing.

One day, when grace pays dividends you didn't expect, you'll realize the that the "R" in ROI was never about return. It was about reimagining what you and your relationships could become, because when you invest in people, eventually, you start seeing *yourself* differently, too. You stop waiting for permission and start recognizing partnerships between you, God, and the opportunities He's already placed within reach.

Real ROI begins with courage—while every relationship, every moment of generosity, every "Let me help you" plants a seed, at some point, you have to pick up the shovel and build something with it. That's the tricky part of growth. Love opens your eyes, yes, but faith still has to move your feet. For me, actually *moving* began with something so small and so ordinary that it barely looked spiritual at all: a single piece of paper that led to a risk I almost didn't take.

You, too, might be standing in front of the door to your next season and thinking that it's locked. But it isn't! It's just waiting for you to knock with what's already in your hand.

CHAPTER 14

How I Turned a Piece of Paper Into a Door Key

It's amazing how much power a single sheet of paper can hold. It doesn't look like faith—it looks like 8½ × 11 inches of "I really hope this works." But sometimes obedience wears office supplies. A résumé, a letter, a leap—call it what you want, but that one small act of movement can become the hinge God uses to swing open a door you didn't even know existed.

That's the wild thing about divine opportunity: it rarely looks divine while you're formatting the margins. You think you're just applying, emailing, asking, trying, but Heaven's already running logistics in the background. This illusion of control gives us that belief that we're steering the ship. Faith calls it partnership out of a realization that the ship was built for storms you didn't know were coming and for the leverage you didn't know you had. Something as small as paper, prayer, and persistence can rewrite an entire story, because doors don't open for the most qualified, they open for the ones who *knock anyway.*

The Myth of the Perfect Résumé

We've all been sold the same corporate fairy tale: get the font right, pick verbs that sound like you run a Fortune 500 company, and *BOOM!* Doors open, angels sing, and LinkedIn endorsements rain down upon you. If résumé-writing were a drinking game for corporate clichés, no one would survive past the second paragraph what with all the instances of "collaborated," "optimized," "managed," and "leveraged."

Reality check: your résumé isn't a spell, it's a signal. It's your attempt to whisper "Hey, I belong here!" in under 400 words. The human brain can decide whether an applicant is a yay or a nay in seven seconds flat. That's thin slicing, or our ability to form lasting judgments off minimal data. Recruiters are Olympic-level thin slicers. (And scanners. They scan more than they read.) They can sense confidence the way a shark senses blood. All of which means that your résumé isn't going to be judged by what you say, but by how it *feels.* Does it tell a story? Does it make you sound like someone who cares? Confidence has a rhythm and belief has a pulse, and when you write from faith instead of fear, people *feel* it. Hence résumés are actually psychological documents that transfer belief.

When recruiters are exercising their significant powers of cognitive efficiency, they're scanning for patterns of *conviction* as opposed to solely evaluating your experiences. Does this person sound like they know who they are, or are they quietly apologizing for existing? Every word, every verb, every line break broadcasts your self-belief or lack thereof. Soft phrases kill energy: "Assisted with…" "Helped manage…" "Supported the team…"

After scanning a few hundred résumés, recruiters start to experience semantic saturation, the psychological phenomenon where a word loses all meaning after you see it too many times. Guess which words are the most overused and hence nearly disappear in front of recruiters' eyes? "Passionate," "motivated," and "team player." They eventually all sound like static on a conference call. That's why the trick isn't to write more, it's to write differently. Novelty activates the brain's anterior cingulate cortex, the part that says, "Wait—this is new! Pay attention." So when you replace "results-oriented" with something specific like "Turned Tuesday chaos into Friday deliverables," you don't just stand out, you *stick.*

Maybe that's divine irony—God made you unique, and then you tried to sound like everyone else to fit in. But Heaven's hiring philosophy has always been the opposite: He blesses the original, not the imitation. When you write your story and include the awkward parts and the weird metaphors no one else would use, you're not oversharing, you're showing proof of life. And when you write with certainty, the reader's mind *feels* your conviction. That's persuasion without selling. That's psychology doing PR for purpose.

Every résumé line should answer two subconscious questions: "Can I trust you?" and "Will you make my life easier?" You can say "Yes!" by showing transformation, not tasks:

✗ Managed social media accounts.
✓ Built a 40,000-person community that turned followers into customers.

✗ Administrative assistant.
✓ Unofficial office therapist, chaos coordinator, and bringer of Starbucks peace offerings.

Your résumé's job is to prove you can *matter*. Mattering is sacred. It's the thread that connects your purpose to the world's problems; it's what turns a job into a calling. So, stop trying to sound corporate and start sounding called. When you write from calling, even a recruiter can feel the peace behind your punctuation. When you stop praying for "the right job" and start preparing to be the right *person*—when you allow your conviction to shine through in your words—your résumé isn't going to open the door, *you* will.

When the Door Doesn't Open

Sometimes you send out forty-seven résumés, and Indeed starts sending you emails like "Still unemployed? Here are twelve more jobs you won't get." Rejection stings. But most of the time, it's just feedback with bad manners. Sometimes the lock wasn't made for your key. Sometimes the lock *was* yours, but the timing wasn't. And sometimes (and this one hurts) God's just protecting you from a door you would've forced open and later regretted walking through.

But here's what neuroscience and scripture agree on: repetition rewires. Every rejection forces your brain to adapt, reinterpret, and redefine meaning. It's called neuroplastic resilience. Each "No" doesn't just bruise your ego, it builds the circuitry you need to handle uncertainty. Every "Not yet" strengthens your emotional immune system. Romans 5:3–4 said it long before LinkedIn did: "Suffering produces perseverance; perseverance, character; and character, hope." That's neuroplasticity in biblical form. Every "no" allows you to strengthen muscles you'll need for the door that *will* open.

Of course, even though you're building up your emotional immune system, rejection still hurts. That's because it triggers the same brain regions that physical pain does—your anterior cingulate cortex is going to light up like a bad Yelp review of your self-worth. That's why rejection feels personal: it *is*, biologically. But reframing it by saying, "This isn't rejection, it's redirection" activates the prefrontal cortex, which is your logic center. That's where peace lives. You can't control the "no," but you *can* control the narrative that follows it.

The Rewrite That Changed Everything

I once applied for a leadership role I had no business getting. Like, I was a "I'll probably need to google what this job actually does" level of unqualified. But this time, I sent a new résumé, one that sounded like a genuine person had written it. Within twenty-four hours, the recruiter called. "I don't usually do this," she said, "but your résumé actually made me smile."

Smile. Dopamine surge. My inner monologue screamed, *Don't ruin this, John!*

She continued, "You just sound like someone I'd want to work with." And that's when it hit me: it was never about perfection, it was about *personality* and *truth.* When I wrote that new résumé, I was honest about what I knew, what I didn't, and who I was becoming. That honesty made me stand out thanks to the vulnerability paradox, which states that people trust you more when you admit imperfection. Why? It signals authenticity.

Along with being more honest in that iteration of my résumé, I had rewritten it as if I were the hiring manager. Instead of "Here's what I did," I wrote, "Here's how I solved the problem." I replaced "responsible for" with "achieved." I turned every bullet into a one-line trailer for the movie of my life and I cut 40% of the fluff. Old line: "Responsible for leading team meetings." New line: "Turned chaotic Monday meetings into 20-minute alignment sessions that saved 4 hours a week." Same facts, but new energy.

A résumé should feel like a short emotional experience of what it's like to work with you and how you can serve your potential employer. Shift from needing to prove yourself to figuring out how you can serve others, because once you start writing from a perspective of service, you stop begging for doors to open and start building your own hinges. When I did that, my résumé wasn't just about getting hired—it was about learning to translate belief into action, to speak the same language that faith had already written on my heart.

The Invisible Lines Recruiters Read Between

Every bullet point in your résumé is a micro-story, and whether you realize it or not, your story reveals your mindset. Each line quietly answers questions like:

- "Do they solve problems or just report them?"
- "Do they take ownership or wait for permission?"
- "Do they think in dots or in connections?"

In other words, recruiters are interpreting your worldview and how *you* think about what you did. If you write "Assisted with a client presentation," that tells recruiters you were there. If you write "Contributed key insights that helped secure a $2M renewal," that tells recruiters you *mattered*. Doors open because someone senses they can trust you, that what you say in your résumé really feels like it's your real life and your real life feels like something you'd be proud to put your name on.

Recruiters might not concretely recognize that as you being in alignment, but they'll feel your calm, grounded energy. In essence, they'll feel your character, which is something that goes beyond competence. And character—both neurologically and spiritually—is magnetic. When your energy is anchored, your résumé doesn't just say "Hire me!", it says, "I can carry weight without crumbling." *That's* the unspoken miracle recruiters are looking for. Degrees and certifications might get you into the room, but only character keeps you there.

> ### WITHIN REACH TOOLKIT
> ### *"Unlock Your Story"*

To get ready to unpack this toolkit, grab a pen, a quiet space, and maybe a snack! Spiritual (and professional) growth burns calories.

Step 1: Identify five moments that mattered.

Not job titles, moments. The ones that still make you smile when you think, *I actually did something there.*

Neuroscience: Recalling specific wins activates your brain's self-efficacy loop. In other words, you'll build confidence through evidence.
Faith Note: Every memory of growth is proof of grace. Those weren't just career wins, they were training grounds.

Step 2: Find the impact.

For each moment, ask "What changed because I was there?" If your absence wouldn't have changed the outcome, dig deeper. This matters because the human brain values impact over activity. God does, too. He's not looking for motion, He's looking for meaning.

Step 3: Translate that impact into résumé language.

Action verb + measurable result + emotional outcome: "Turned chaos into clarity that saved 4 hours a week."

Neuroscience: Specific verbs calm the brain.
Faith Note: Specific gratitude opens the heart.

Step 4: Rehearse out loud.

Read your résumé out loud. If it sounds like a deposition, rewrite it until it sounds like brunch with purpose. Reading it aloud will activate your mirror neurons, the same ones recruiters use to "feel" your energy.

Faith Note: Speaking your story aloud is a form of declaration. Heaven loves confidence wrapped in humility.

Step 5: Align your platforms.

Your résumé, LinkedIn, interview stories—they should all sound like the same human wrote them.

Neuroscience: Consistency breeds trust.
Faith Note: Consistency is just integrity in motion. It tells the world, "I am the same person on paper, online, and when no one's watching."

Step 6: The résumé decoder.

Highlight tasks in yellow and impact in green. If the page looks like lemonade, start squeezing for more meaning.

Neuroscience: Our brains scan for cause and effect.
Faith Note: Heaven does, too: "By their fruit, you'll know them." (Matthew 7:16)

Step 7: The impact map.

Left side: your contribution. Right side: the emotion it created (relief, pride, hope, peace, etc.).

Neuroscience: Emotion doubles memory retention.
Faith Note: Emotion is energy in motion—it's how the Spirit leaves fingerprints on your work.

Step 8: The mirror draft.

Write one résumé no one will ever read—the raw, honest one. Then compare it to your polished version. That gap? That's where your authenticity got edited out. Close the gap. Because God can't bless the fake version of you that you're trying to sell.

Step 9: Your confidence formula.

Confidence = evidence × exposure. Every time you do something good, that's evidence. Every time you let it be seen, that's exposure. You don't inspire trust by hiding your gifts! Even humility needs marketing sometimes. Let your light *shine*, not shrink.

Step 10: Rewrite the ending.

Ask yourself, "What story do I want this next résumé to tell about who I'm becoming?" Then write the first paragraph. Start with "I'm becoming the kind of person who…" That line will become your compass for your job search, your habits, and your prayers. Because this whole chapter was never about *paper,* it was about *permission*. Permission to believe that the God who gave you gifts didn't intend for you to hide them behind bullet points.

The résumé gets you noticed. Your energy gets you trusted. Your story gets you remembered. Your faith gets you placed exactly where you're meant to be. When all four align, that's not coincidence, that's calling. And that's when doors don't just open, they *swing wide.*

When Paper Meets Providence

Every story has a plot twist that doesn't make sense until you rewind it. For me, a big twist started in the least glamorous place imaginable: a cluttered webpage full of sketchy job listings, broken links, and way too many "opportunities" that sounded like pyramid schemes. But somewhere in that digital chaos, God was hiding my next assignment. It only took a single click to reroute my entire life.

CHAPTER 15

How Craigslist Defined the Trajectory of My Entire Career

My plot twist began on Craigslist. Not on LinkedIn or with a recruiter. Not divine thunder from the heavens. Just a sketchy-looking job post sandwiched between a used treadmill and someone selling "lightly worn" ferrets. On top of that, I wasn't searching for destiny, I was just searching for rent money. But that's the thing about God—He'll use whatever tab you have open. One click, one email, one small act of desperation disguised as curiosity was all it took. In hindsight, that "random" scroll wasn't random at all, of course. It was strategy wearing bad web design.

You've probably heard of this kind of small-action-leading-to-big-plot-twist as the butterfly effect. In short, small actions can create massive ripple impacts. Faith calls it divine orchestration—it's a subtle reminder that purpose doesn't need your perfect plan, just your participation. When you're in alignment, it's a lot more about finding the right opportunity in the most unlikely places than it is about luck.

Welcome to California!

When I first arrived in California, I didn't know a soul. When I dropped my mom off at the airport for her flight back to Ohio, she gave me that worried-but-supportive look moms reserve for "He swears he's fine" moments. I gave her a hug and told her I loved her and she headed into the airport.

As I drove away, it hit me: I was *really* there. No safety net. No soft landing. Just a big sky, bigger rent, and a dream with wobbly legs. That night, sitting on an air mattress that sounded like a bag of chips every time I exhaled, I had one of those "God, are You sure?" conversations. Although I didn't hear a voice, I felt something settle in my chest, the kind of quiet peace that says, "Faith is believing long before the proof of belief is present." Faith is about motion, not certainty. It's about trusting that even if the GPS is glitching, the signal's still good.

But two weeks into "chasing my gold," the GPS was still glitching: I still didn't have any apartment, so everything I owned was in the car—and that car was in a Target parking lot. The dinner menu was McDonald's dollar menu. My parents called me nightly and kept begging me to come home. Part of me wanted to, because turning back is always easier than looking fear in the face. But I knew if I left then, I'd never come back. My dream would die quietly in the back seat next to the box fan. So, I did the thing that would become my unofficial life motto: I chose the hard, on purpose.

Homeless. Jobless. Terrified. And yet, weirdly, I wasn't alone. It's funny how faith sometimes looks like exhaustion with good posture. I remember staring out the windshield one night, praying through the steering wheel like it was a confessional. "God, I don't need a miracle. Just a direction." And I swear I heard the faintest whisper: "Forward." That one word became oxygen.

If I wanted to find my gold, the one God had put on my map, retreat wasn't an option. In fact, according to the strange math of growth, in the moments when you feel the most hopeless, you often find momentum by running toward the very thing that scares you. Looking back, that Target parking lot was less of a failure and more of a furnace that was burning off the parts of me that depended on comfort instead of calling.

The Marketplace of Questionable Life Choices

Craigslist: the original Wild West of the Internet, half job board, half psychological experiment. A place where dreams, scams, and divine appointments all share a homepage. You can buy a used Honda, a ferret, and a "lightly haunted" couch in the same scroll.

I clicked on Jobs. My plan was to find a bartending gig. College had taught me two things: how to pour drinks and how to pretend to care about people's problems. (In hindsight, that was early leadership training.) Then I saw it: SoCalGas. A real company! With benefits! Health insurance that didn't start with "GoFund" and end with "Me." The role? Analyst. And miracle of miracles, I'd had one co-op semester of doing exactly that. For once, I wasn't wildly unqualified for something I actually wanted.

I applied. The application was through a staffing agency. Enter Jan, a recruiter who could spot potential in a half-deflated balloon. She looked at me—nervous, over-caffeinated, underqualified—and decided I was bet-worthy. She then proceeded to build my résumé from scratch. No Canva—just Microsoft Word and faith.

"Smile!" was her advice when I went to do the interview. "Be yourself. Also, maybe don't mention you found this between ferrets and futons." Somehow, sweat stains and all, I got the job. No confetti cannon. No inspirational soundtrack. Just quiet gratitude and a strong suspicion that Heaven had just flexed its networking department muscles.

For sixteen years, SoCalGas became my proving ground, providing me with structure, systems, and psychological safety, the latter because people do their best work when they're not afraid of learning in front of others. But there was something deeper happening under the TPS reports and status meetings: God was teaching me patience disguised as process. He doesn't rush purpose, He refines it.

I used to think calling meant clarity, but really, calling often looks like consistency: showing up every day to the same cubicle, the same challenges, and the same coffee stains and trusting that none of it is a waste of your time.

There's a quirk in our brains called serendipity bias. That's when we look back at random events and assign them meaning like they were part of a grand design. But maybe they *were*. "Chance favors the prepared mind," Pasteur said. Behavioral science adds: "...and the moving feet." It's a neurological fact that action flips on your reticular activating system (RAS), which is the brain's filter for what matters. Once you activate it, your brain starts spotting dots you can connect.

It's not luck, it's neuroplasticity meeting divine choreography. In that same vein, for me, Craigslist wasn't destiny, it was obedience. It was an imperfect step toward a future that, in hindsight, was everything.

Even if you've never scoured Craigslist for a job, every career has a Craigslist moment: the day when curiosity beats certainty. That's agency activation, a.k.a. the instant your nervous system shifts from helpless to hopeful. When you act, you tell your body, "We're not stuck, we're starting." That's when Heaven tends to slide the next breadcrumb across the table. That's momentum. That's neuroscience. That's faith in motion. So, don't wait to feel qualified, just get into the room! Your résumé doesn't have to be perfect, your obedience does.

Another truth of life is that all things eventually come to an end. After sixteen years, the SoCalGas chapter of my life ended quietly. No slow clap, no farewell tour, just clarity: it was time. Walking away hurt—endings always do—but it reminded me that the same stubborn courage I'd found in a Target parking lot was still in me.

WITHIN REACH TOOLKIT
The Serendipity Engine

Our brains backfill meaning after we've made progress, not before it. When we move, we give our mind (and our Maker) material to work with. Action primes the RAS to notice opportunity and cues the prefrontal cortex to plan and persist. Motion tells the brain "This is important!" and faith replies "Copy—I'll find more of that." Which is why luck doesn't happen *to* you, it happens *through* you when preparation meets providence.

Here's how to turn chaos into career breakthroughs (and maybe strengthen your prayer life while you're at it):

1) Follow breadcrumbs, not blueprints.

Forget the 10-year plan! Make a 10-minute one. Curiosity is your GPS; consistency is the engine. Start. Adjust. Repeat.

2) The luck equation = P × M × O.

Luck = Preparation × Motion × Openness. Study the game (P). Play the game (M). Say yes to odd invites (O). God does some of His best work in "accidental" meetings.

3) Rehearse readiness (micro-dares).

Confidence follows evidence, so do one small scary thing daily: one

DM, one call, one ask. Track what happens. Your amygdala chills out when your calendar proves you survived.

4) Reframe rejection.

"No" isn't a wall, it's a wayfinding sign. Extract the intel: timing, pitch, target. Iterate, don't internalize. Even Jesus got rejected in His hometown. You'll live.

5) Keep a serendipity journal.

Log every "lucky" break for 30 days. Note what you did right before it happened. You'll discover your "luck patterns" have God's fingerprints all over them.

6) Reflect on these questions:

- What's one random or risky decision that redirected your life?
- How did curiosity or desperation play a role?
- If you trusted the breadcrumbs again, what could your next Craigslist moment look like this week?

Sometimes the universe doesn't send a map—it sends a parking lot, a Craigslist link, and a stubborn sense of "not yet." Fortunately, your job isn't to predict the path. Your job is to keep moving faithfully, awkwardly, and purposefully. Because every full-circle story starts with one imperfect step.

When the Door Actually Opens

It's one thing to find an opportunity, but it's quite another to show up for it with confidence, composure, and maybe a little divine calmness supplementing your caffeine. While favor might open the door, preparation decides how long you get to stay inside. It's time to stop memorizing lines and start mastering presence, a.k.a. the subtle art of walking into a room knowing that you already belong there.

CHAPTER 16

The Strategy That Moves You From Candidate to No-Brainer

There's nothing quite like the adrenaline of an interview, that sacred intersection where ambition meets flop sweat. You're trying to look calm while your inner voice is quoting Philippians 4:13 like it's a panic-button mantra: "I can do all things through Christ who strengthens me…including making eye contact for thirty minutes." The waiting room always feels like a psychological experiment, where everyone is pretending they didn't google "top 10 interview questions" last night. But the real test starts long before the handshake—it starts with the story your presence is already telling.

I used to think interviews were about answering questions, but really, they're about answering *energy*. That gets us back to thin-slicing, the brain's ability to make lightning-fast judgments based on micro-cues. A posture that instantly says "I'm not here to prove I belong, I'm here because I *do* belong" changes everything. You want your peaceful presence to make the room believe you before you've even finished your sentence.

The Illusion of Knowing What You're Doing

Let's get one universal truth out of the way: no one, and I mean *no one*, walks into an interview fully knowing what they're doing. Not the college grad rehearsing answers in the bathroom mirror. Not the mid-level pro with "10+ years of experience" (translation: 10+ years of winging it with conviction). And definitely not the person interviewing you—they've just had more practice pretending that they do.

When I first started interviewing, I thought confidence meant having *every* answer ready to go. So naturally, I turned into a human flash drive and memorized every possible question the internet could invent: "Tell me about a time you faced conflict" and "Where do you see yourself in five years?" and "If you were a kitchen utensil, which one would you be?" (I said, "Spatula, because I'm flexible under pressure." The interviewer did *not* laugh. My soul left my body.)

Every interview, I would walk in sweating caffeine and desperation, gripping my résumé like it was a sacred scroll. My smile said "confident," but my hands were performing a full Pentecostal praise session under the table. Later, I realized something painfully liberating: the only interview hack that *actually* works is delusional confidence. Not the "I'm gonna sell everything and start a llama farm" kind, but the kind that whispers, "Hey, I belong here, even if we're still catching up to that truth."

Practice confidence first—competence will catch up later. That might sound delusional, but the best kind of faith always does. Because honestly, nobody *really* knows what they're doing. Some people are just better at acting calm while secretly praying under their breath that God will give them the right next word.

Of course, "Fake it till you make it" sounds cute until you're faking it in front of someone whose job is literally to detect fakes. This unfortunate truth hit me when early in my career, someone asked me, "Would you describe yourself as a natural leader?"

Without hesitation, I said, "Absolutely."

She smiled. "Great! Tell me about a time you led a team."

And my brain froze like an app that needed an update. "Uh... I convinced my group chat to switch from WhatsApp to iMessage?"

Yeah. Bold start. Weak finish.

That was when I learned the difference between pretending and *translating.* Confidence isn't about lying, it's about connecting dots that don't look connected yet. You take the puzzle pieces of your life—your side hustles, your awkward projects, your "This probably doesn't count" moments—and reframe them as proof that you can lead. You're not saying, "I've done this exact thing before," you're saying, "I've done *things like this* before, and I'll do it again, and better."

Confidence is essentially a translator: it helps people finally see who you've been becoming. It's like faith in the sense that you're trusting that what doesn't make sense yet will make sense later. You're not faking it, you're framing it! And that's the real hack: confidence is repurposing evidence.

Let's nerd out for a second and check out the science behind this. Your brain has a built-in security guard called the amygdala. Its job is to detect danger, but it has a flaw, namely terrible pattern recognition. To your amygdala, a job interview feels the same as being chased by a bear in business casual: heart racing, palms sweating, voice cracking. Meanwhile, your prefrontal cortex, the brain's overworked therapist, is like, "Relax. It's not a bear. It's Brenda from HR."

Delusional confidence is how you hack that system. You feed your nervous system a new story: "We've done hard things before! We can handle this, too." This works because your brain doesn't care whether confidence is real—it only cares whether it's repeated. When you act confident, your body releases the same neurochemicals that it would if you actually *were* confident. Fake it long enough, then, and your biology catches up. That's why visualization, affirmations, and "power posing" aren't just motivational fluff, they're neuroscience in drag. You're tricking your amygdala into thinking you belong until it stops sending panic memos.

In a nutshell, confidence is a trained response. Which is great news, because you don't need to wait for it to appear—you can practice it until your nervous system gets bored of panicking. If you want a little extra boost, just remember Who wired that nervous system in the first place. If He designed your brain to adapt, maybe He also designed that fear to fade once you start showing up anyway.

Interviewee and Interviewer

My first real interview was in a fifty-story building named after the company I was interviewing for. I wore a tie so tight it felt like I was choking on my own ambition. When they asked, "Why do you want to work here?", I said, "Because…you're hiring and I need money?" Iconic response.

Those early interviews were chaos, but sacred chaos. They humbled me faster than any self-help book ever could have, because I realized the managers were hiring for potential, not perfection. Managers don't want robots who memorize scripts—they want humans who can adapt.

One hiring manager told me, "I don't hire the most qualified person. I hire the most coachable." That line hit me like divine wisdom disguised as business advice. It made me stop chasing flawless answers and start chasing honest ones. That was when it clicked: an interview is an energy exchange. And your presence walks into the room fifteen seconds before you do, so show up with peace, not panic, because sometimes what's most noticeable about you isn't what you say, it's what you *carry.*

Fast-forward a few years, and suddenly, I was the one asking the questions. Wild. *Me,* the guy who had once said "Spatula" with conviction, was now sitting across the table holding someone's future like it was a hot cup of coffee I didn't want to spill. You'd think that would've made me feel powerful, but it didn't—it made me feel protective. Because I could see the invisible weight every candidate was carrying: the student loans, the self-doubt, the "Please, God, let this go well" prayer whispered under shaky breath.

Really, though, interviewers just want to meet someone who makes them think, *If I hire this person, my job will get easier, and maybe, just maybe, I'll finally sleep through the night.* In short, they want relief. They want somebody who has a calm presence. And that's it. That's the whole game.

Once I was the one sitting on the hiring side of the desk, I could tell within five minutes who was acting confident and who was owning calm. The difference was clear: acting confident is performance, while owning calm is peace. The first fills the room; the second steadies it. And the steady one always wins. Calmness, confidence, humility, humor, curiosity—those are the currencies that buy trust.

Your presence either tightens the room or lightens it. People who are pros at interviewing walk in like they trust the process because they trust the One who wired them for the room they're in. He also prepared the room for *your* arrival.

All of that said, there's a big difference between *healthy delusion* (a.k.a. confidence) and whatever Elon Musk wakes up believing some mornings. Healthy delusion whispers, "I may not know everything, but I'll learn faster than anyone." Hazardous delusion screams, "Who needs med school? I watched *Grey's Anatomy!*"

Here's my personal filter for confidence: "Would my future self thank me for this level of confidence?" If the answer's yes, I lean in. If the answer's "My future self would probably sue me," I step back.

Confidence without competence is chaos in a suit. Competence without confidence is invisibility. But a balance of both? That's *credibility.* And credibility isn't built by being flawless, it's built by being *faithful.* People remember less about what you said and more about whether you did what you said you'd do. That's how healthy delusion becomes *trust:* it's repeated evidence that your follow-through matches your faith.

Jobs You Aren't Qualified For and Interviews You Don't Expect

I once applied for a job that required ten years of experience. I had... well, let's just say much less. (But to be fair, I've never been very good at details like following directions.) Every bullet point on that posting screamed, "You're not enough!" And for a split second, I believed it. But then I thought, *Half of this job description is just corporate poetry for common sense,* so I applied anyway.

Did I get it? No. Did I get something better? Absolutely: a mentor. Who called me later and said, "You weren't the most qualified, but you *were* the most memorable."

That one line rewired my entire outlook. Because the goal isn't to win every interview, the goal is to leave a mental fingerprint that lingers. Every "no" is still data. Every "almost" is still progress. And every "You're not ready yet" secretly means "You're already on the radar."

God doesn't waste rejection, He recycles it. What you think is a closed door is usually a redirection to a hallway you didn't even know existed yet. All of those rejections—especially the ones that sting—prepare you for the next opportunity. Your only job is to stay curious long enough to connect the dots later, because eventually, life flips the script. The interviews stop being scheduled and start being spontaneous—now they happen in hallways, Slack threads, and coffee lines. Someone asks, "How are things going?", and BOOM! Interview. Someone introduces you at an event. Interview. Someone watches how you treat the intern, and that's the real interview.

When you get down to it, *everything* is an interview in some way. People are always quietly evaluating things that never appear on a job description. How do you handle stress? Do you give credit or hoard it? Do you show up the same when no one's watching? Ironically, most people prep for the least important interviews (the scheduled ones) and ignore the ones that actually define their reputation.

People remember *energy.* They remember the way others made them feel safe, seen, or inspired. So, the next time life seemingly catches you off guard, remember that it's not an ambush. It's just another divine audition for alignment. Favor doesn't announce itself on your calendar—it checks how you carry yourself when you think no one's watching.

Confidence vs. Arrogance

There's a razor-thin line between confidence and arrogance, and most people find it by tripping over it in front of HR. Arrogance says: "I already know." Confidence says: "I can figure it out." Arrogance performs; confidence connects. Arrogance walks into an interview to *impress,* while confidence walks in to *align.*

The most magnetic people don't need to shout their worth—they just radiate it. They know exactly who they are, and maybe more importantly, who they're not *yet.* Psychologists call this idea that everyone can see how nervous you are the illusion of transparency. "Illusion" because they don't see your anxiety—they see your *intent.*

So, walk in like someone who trusts that you're placed there on purpose, not by accident. Say, "I'm here to learn, contribute, and grow." That energy speaks louder than your résumé ever could. And remember that confidence isn't the absence of fear—it's the decision to speak anyway and not be invisible. It's not letting yourself shrink so that you don't seem "too much." Confidence is having *clarity* about who you are and what you're there to do.

Confidence is also a daily decision. It's the quiet whisper before the big moment that says "I belong here" even when the room feels too big. It's the humor that diffuses fear; it's the grace that keeps you grounded even when your plans fall apart in public. If anyone asks how you became confident, tell them the truth: "I didn't. I just kept showing up until my nervous system got bored of being scared."

So, breathe. Straighten your posture. Crack a joke. Say a quiet prayer. And walk into that room like someone who knows that even if you don't land this one, you're still being led somewhere better.

When Imposter Syndrome Pulls Up a Chair

Imposter syndrome never really leaves, it just changes disguises. Early career version: "Am I good enough to get this job?" Leadership version: "Am I good enough to lead these people?" Same voice, bigger consequences. But here's the cosmic joke: the people who question themselves the most are usually the ones *most* qualified to lead. Fakes don't have imposter syndrome. They *should*, but they don't.

That inner critic in your head isn't your enemy, it's your editor. It's the reminder that you care enough to do better. Once I realized that, I stopped trying to silence mine—now when that voice shows up before a big moment, I tell it, "Hey, you can stay, but sit quietly in the back while my boy Confidence runs the show." (Sometimes I say that out loud, and yes, people stare. Yes, it works. No, I don't care.) Feeling underqualified doesn't mean you're behind, it means you're growing. And if you ever doubt that, remember, God doesn't call the qualified. He qualifies the called.

To get to the physiological heart of the matter, though, we have to talk about our nervous system. Every time anybody walks into an interview, their body runs a full diagnostic: "Are we safe? Are we seen? Are we about to be emotionally vaporized by Amy's follow-up question?" Our posture, tone, and breathing all send real-time status reports to our brain, and our brain listens. That's why micro-confidence cues matter. Next time you walk into a room, try doing this:

- Set your shoulders back. That tells your body, "We've got this."
- Slowly exhale. That drops your heart rate and raises your authority.
- Smile, even if it's a tiny smile. That signals your brain, "We're not dying, we're just talking to Amy."

Remind your body that it's safe! Your spirit already knows it's covered. When you walk in trusting that you're not alone in the room, your biology will follow suit. Peace is chemistry baptized in perspective. Your body builds a résumé long before you print one, so teach it how to walk in calmly.

The Reframe and the Follow-Up

Reframing is psychological aikido: it uses your fear's momentum against itself. You don't deny the nerves, you redirect them. Let's play this out:

FEAR THOUGHT	REFRAME THOUGHT
"I'm not ready."	"I'm about to level up."
"They're judging me."	"We're just seeing if we fit each other."
"What if I fail?"	"What if this is the rep before the win?"

When you reframe a situation, you're not lying to yourself, you're upgrading the narrative. Your brain is always telling a story, and *you* get to choose whether it's a tragedy or a comeback. But you don't have to control every outcome when you trust the Author. Your job is to just stay in character when the story gets weird—a plot twist is coming, and it'll be a good one. Your body, mind, and spirit are all going to believe whichever story you tell most often, so give them a story worth rehearsing.

Part of reframing is following up. *Not* sending the 2 a.m. thank-you email that sounds like ChatGPT and Google Docs had a baby, but something that sounds human, like, "Hey, I really appreciated our conversation, especially the part about [insert actual thing you remember]. I left even more excited about how I could contribute to [insert mission or value that resonated]."

That's it. Simple. Real. Sincere. Psychologically, that follow-up email will trigger the reciprocity bias: people feel more connected to those who make *them* feel seen. Spiritually, it's just good stewardship—you're honoring the opportunity, not begging for it.

But even though following up is easy, still, most people never do it. Which means the ones who do instantly rise above the noise. A thoughtful follow-up says, "I noticed. I care. I'll do the same once I'm on your team." *That's* the kind of energy that turns strangers into advocates.

The D.E.L.U.S.I.O.N. Framework

You knew it was coming: an acronym so confident that it basically walked into this chapter uninvited:

PRINCIPLE	DESCRIPTION
D: Define your story	Have three or four personal stories ready to tell that show growth, grit, and grace. Perfect is boring; progress sells.
E: Energy management	Your breath, your pace, your posture—they all set the vibe. You don't enter a room, you tune it.
L: Listen actively	Confidence isn't volume, it's presence. Listening like you mean it is your secret flex.
U: Unlearn scripts	Drop the robotic "team player" lines. Replace them with the real you. Real beats rehearsed every time.
S: Signal curiosity	Ask sharp questions about vision, impact, and purpose. Do not ask, "So, what's the pay?" (Yet.)
I: Imposter reframing	When doubt shows up, treat it like data: proof you're stretching, not failing.
O: Own your calm	Silence is power. Pauses build trust. Your peace is your credibility.
N: Normalize nerves	Everyone's heart races, so make yours beat with purpose. Channel adrenaline into awareness.

Delusion, redefined, is belief strong enough to bend reality in your direction. Or in faith terms: seeing the unseen until it shows up. Because maybe confidence isn't about believing in yourself, maybe it's about believing you were sent. And that's not delusion. That's design.

The Post-Interview Spiral (and How to Survive It)

Five minutes after every interview, we all become forensic analysts, wondering, *Did I talk too much? Did I talk too little? Did I weirdly compliment their office plant?* This post-interview spiral is just our brain trying to close an open loop. It hates uncertainty! It wants closure, validation, or at least an email that says, "You didn't totally embarrass yourself."

The antidote isn't to suppress the spiral, it's to give it *structure.* Try this quick-reset ritual:

1. Write down one thing that worked.
2. Write down one thing that didn't.
3. Write down one thing to try next time.

Then close the mental tab and move on. Growth doesn't hate failure, it feeds on it. Every cringe moment is data. Every rejection is redirection, often before you even realize what it's redirecting you *toward.* So, stop treating silence like failure. Sometimes God's "not yet" sounds a lot like no reply.

WITHIN REACH TOOLKIT
Confidence Reality Check

Let's turn this chapter into motion with these practices:

1. The three-moment mirror test.

Write down three times you felt underqualified but succeeded anyway. Next to each, list the mindset or miracle that carried you through. That's your confidence DNA, proof you've done hard things before *with help bigger than you.*

2. Fear reframe worksheet.

Take one current fear and complete this sentence:

"If I handled ____, then I can handle this." Read it out loud. Notice how your shoulders drop when faith replaces fiction.

3. 90-second power reset

Before your next interview or presentation:

- Inhale for 4.
- Hold for 4.
- Exhale for 4.
- Hold for 4.
- Smile for 1.

It's a neurological reset: your amygdala chills out and your confidence clocks in.

4. The rewatch rule.

Record yourself answering a tough question. Watch it back, not to critique, but to *coach*. Confidence isn't built in mirrors; it's built in replays.

5. The follow-up habit.

Within 24 hours, send a genuine follow-up message that mentions one specific moment from your conversation. That encore will often become the seed for your next opportunity.

Confidence isn't loud. It's not a performance. It's the muscle memory of self-trust built one small reach at a time. If you listen closely, underneath the nerves, the doubt, the shaky small talk, you'll hear it: that steady heartbeat whispering, "You've done hard things before. You can do this, too." That's not delusion, that's data. That's divine design.

When Confidence Meets Communication

People don't remember what you said, they remember how you made them *feel.* You can deliver the most flawless résumé summary and list every quantifiable metric known to LinkedIn, yet still lose the room to someone who simply told a better story. That's because even though numbers build credibility, stories build connection. One satisfies logic and the other awakens empathy. Humans buy, hire, and follow from the heart first and the brain second. Stories *transform.* Stories open hearts. That's where real influence begins.

CHAPTER 17

How to Move Minds, Shift Hearts, and Actually Make People Care

Interviews, meetings, pitches, even conversations with your boss are all just chapters of the same book titled *The Story of You.* If you don't learn to tell it, someone else will summarize it for you. Probably badly. On the other hand, if you can tell your story well—if you can engage others in narrative transportation, which is when someone gets so absorbed in your story that their brain stops judging and starts *experiencing*—then people will love your story.

Nothing travels faster through the human heart than honesty wrapped in a little vulnerability. When you know how to communicate in a way that moves people and when you can turn data into dialogue, your message will sound like it has a soul again. Your story will make people remember why you were there.

The Gospel of Storytelling (According to Your Amygdala)

If your story starts with, "It all began when corporate sent an email," I've already spiritually left the room. Stories are emotional transactions, and your audience consists of caffeinated, overstimulated, emotionally dehydrated creatures trying to make sense of themselves between emails, errands, and existential dread. Telling an interview about yourself in a listicle, monotone kind of way won't get you noticed.

Or maybe you already *are* that one person who can describe a parallel parking experience in a truly gripping, Oscar-worthy way. People who can pull that off aren't necessarily better speakers, they're better feelers. Facts get remembered; *feelings* get repeated. And repetition is what turns a story into influence. So, if you want to be unforgettable in your career, in your relationships, in the moment when your boss asks you to "say a few words" and you accidentally give a TED Talk, then stop reporting your life and start reliving it. Let people see your heartbeat, not your highlight reel. Let them recognize their own story in yours.

When you tell a story, your listener's brain doesn't just hear it, it *recreates* it. That's thanks to those super-helpful mirror neurons, a.k.a. your empathy Wi-Fi. When you describe the terror of being called on in a meeting you weren't prepared for, your listeners' palms sweat, too. When you talk about landing your dream job, their own dopamine spikes. When you admit you cried in your car after pretending you were "fine," they feel that ache with you. All because you're not communicating, you're *co-feeling.*

Data doesn't activate the same system. Facts live in your prefrontal cortex, your brain's spreadsheet. Emotion lives in the amygdala, your brain's panic button. And the amygdala always wins, because feeling is your brain's native language. That's why your audience doesn't perk up when you say, "Our team increased Q3 deliverable efficiency by 14%." They perk up when you say, "We almost didn't make it, and that's what changed everything."

It's the same reason you can't talk your friend out of texting their walking-red-flag ex using logic. You can quote statistics, cite heartbreak timelines, even present a PowerPoint of past mistakes, and none of that will matter. Logic takes a back seat in decision-making—we *feel*, we act, and then we build the logic afterward to justify our questionable life choices. The exchange rate is simple: one authentic emotion equals one unforgettable connection. And that's what we want: to identify with ourselves and with others. Great storytellers generate feelings and let other people see themselves in their story.

Now let's talk about corporate storytelling, the place where emotion goes to die. You know Brian. Every office has a Brian who says something like, "We achieved a 15% efficiency increase leveraging cross-functional synergy." Cool, Brian. But did anyone feel anything? No, because corporate storytelling often removes the very ingredient that makes stories persuasive: *humanity.*

Thanks to cognitive fluency, when you strip emotion to sound "professional," you remove the part of your message that actually persuades. (Cognitive fluency says that if something feels easy to process, people trust it more.) The more human you sound, the more believable you are, so instead of quoting dry statistics, try saying, "We saved $2 million last quarter, but what I'm proud of is how our team stopped blaming each other and started believing in each other."

One of my mentors referred to this as the "Tell me the 'So what?' regarding the numbers." That was the missing piece I needed to connect the numbers with the purpose. The "So what?" is the difference between metrics and meaning, between sounding smart and being heard.

WITHIN REACH TOOLKIT
Be a Better Storyteller

Not everyone nails storytelling. There's a Hall of Fame for storytelling gone wrong:

- **The Rambler:** Started a story in 1999, still talking.
- **The Historian:** Believes "backstory" means "from birth."
- **The Hero Complex:** Every story is about how amazing they are.
- **The PowerPoint Priest:** Thinks charts are emotions.
- **The Trauma Dump Truck:** Confuses vulnerability with venting.

The cure for all of these uninspiring styles is intentionality. Before you tell a story, ask:

- What do I want my audience to feel?
- What do I want them to remember?
- What do I want them to do?

If you can't answer those three, it's not a story, it's a monologue looking for meaning.

Here's another framework I live by: Frame it. Feel it. Finish it.

- **Frame it fast.** Set context and conflict by starting the story where something changed. That triggers dopamine and focus.
- **Feel it deeply.** Use sensory details, not summaries. Details activate mirror neurons and empathy.
- **Finish it intentionally.** Land on insight, not ego. Anchor emotion in meaning so that it sticks.

And before you share a story, check your emotional intent: Who's this for? What are they supposed to feel? Is your vulnerability intentional or indulgent? If your story isn't going to help them, it's probably therapy you didn't pay for.

Attention, Honesty, and Charisma: Humanity's New Currencies

In the modern world, attention is the new currency, and everyone's broke. Every text, post, and presentation is basically begging, "Hey, can I borrow thirty seconds of your brain before it doomscrolls away?" If your story pays back that attention with curiosity, laughter, or goosebumps, that's profit. If it pays back in boredom, you've just emotionally defaulted on your audience, because our brain has about three seconds before it opens Instagram.

So, hook the amygdala before it checks out. Start with tension, humor, or controlled chaos: "I bombed a presentation so badly my boss asked if I was okay afterward, and honestly, I wasn't. Spiritually or emotionally." *BOOM!* You've got the brain's attention. Then feed the mirror neurons. Don't say "I was nervous," show it. Let your audience feel the shaky voice, the sweaty palms, the mental Windows 98 crash.

Finally, anchor the prefrontal cortex by giving people a landing pad. End with a universal takeaway like, "That day taught me that confidence isn't certainty, it's courage on a deadline." That's the trifecta: attention, connection, insight. Hit all three, and your story doesn't just land, it'll linger. But! Part of sticking the landing is *not* making yourself the main character. The moment you stop trying to be the hero, you'll actually become one.

That might seem counterintuitive, but it isn't. Why? People connect to stories that make them feel seen, not ones that just make the storyteller sound perfect. Sure, when you share your highlight reel, they'll admire you...but when you share your blooper reel, they'll *relate* to you. That's called the vulnerability loop: when you're honest, your audience's brain releases oxytocin, the trust chemical. Honesty is contagious. If you say, "I had no idea what I was doing but I did it anyway," then suddenly everyone's rooting for you. Underdogs win. Comebacks sell. Redemption arcs trend. That's not marketing, that's human nature. You don't need to be perfect, you just need to be real enough for someone else's spirit to whisper, "Same."

I saw this scenario play out with a woman I'll call Kayla. She prepped for her dream job interview like it was a NASA launch: flashcards, mock interviews, three shots of espresso and one whispered prayer. She walked into the interview ready to prove she was "a strategic, results-oriented problem solver." She had obviously memorized the vocabulary of LinkedIn.

Then came the heart-stopping question: "Tell me about a time you failed." You could almost hear the Windows error sound playing in her brain. She froze. Then she did something she hadn't practiced: she told the truth. The project that tanked. The nights she stayed late fixing her mistakes. The day she realized leadership wasn't about being the smartest person in the room but being the one who owned it when things went wrong. Her voice cracked.

The interviewer leaned forward and said, "That's the kind of self-awareness we need."

She got the job, not because of her facts, but because of her *feelings.* Vulnerability activates empathy; honesty activates favor. If you think about it, you've probably forgotten most of the facts people have told you, but you still remember how they made you feel. That's because emotion tags your memories — when something makes you laugh, cry, or cringe, your amygdala emails your hippocampus: "Hey, save this one. This matters." That's why you can still remember movie scenes from a decade ago but you can't recall what you had for breakfast this morning.

So, if you want your story to stick, make it emotional. Add sensory texture. Don't say, "I was nervous." Say, "My stomach was auditioning for Cirque du Soleil while my brain was buffering like bad Wi-Fi." Laughter releases dopamine, the "please keep talking" chemical. People listen longer, trust faster, and remember better when they laugh. Humor is holy because it connects hearts faster than logic ever could.

Charisma, too, connects. Fortunately, charisma isn't magic, it's math: Charisma = Authenticity × Energy × Empathy. Charismatic people don't dominate conversations; they use humor to break tension, mirror body language, and match energy with empathy. Charisma is resonance, when someone's words feel like a mirror instead of a microphone. When two nervous systems sync up, that's interpersonal synchrony. The faith translation is fellowship. Either way, it's the moment when someone's presence makes your soul exhale.

The Real Leadership Formula

Here's how the brain decides anything: Emotion → Action → Logic. You feel first. Then you act. Then you come up with a reason that makes your action sound intelligent. That's why storytelling works—it speaks to the emotional sequence before the logical one.

Leadership works the same way. Great leaders don't just communicate tasks, they translate emotion. They turn "What we're doing" into "Why it matters." When a leader says, "We're not just building infrastructure, we're connecting communities," it activates the brain's meaning network. Suddenly, people aren't working *for* them, they're working *with* them. With each other. People follow *inspiration* better than they follow instructions, and inspiration lives where vision meets vulnerability.

The best leaders harvest their scars and turn them into stories. They don't speak to impress, they speak to connect and be *present.*

When the Story Starts Starring *You*

After spending all that time learning how to tell better stories, I did what any overconfident twenty-something would do: I decided to *be* one. Once you realize the power of story, you start wondering what it'd be like to live one worth telling. So I traded boardrooms for casting calls and PowerPoints for monologues, and somehow I ended up auditioning for roles that included "bridesmaid's ex" and "guy in background who nods with intensity." While my acting career never quite made it past "craft services," what it lacked in red carpets, it made up for in revelation.

Chasing a dream that doesn't pan out still teaches you things that success never could. You learn humility, resilience, and the fine art of pretending to understand a director who says things like, "Give me more existential tension with your eyebrows." Psychologists call it growth through failure experiential learning. Faith calls it refinement—it's God teaching you through detours what you refused to learn on the main road.

CHAPTER 18

My Acting Origin Story

Most people love a superhero origin story, that messy middle before the montage. The part where the "before" picture doesn't yet realize it's training for an "after." What fire had to burn off the ego? What heartbreak or rejection rewired their brain for resilience? Psychology calls this post-traumatic growth. It's the divine remix God puts on your pain when you let Him DJ your character development.

Ever since 2008, Iron Man has been my favorite superhero. Tony Stark isn't perfect, but he's confident, funny, and charismatic, and once he builds the suit, he amplifies his impact. He doesn't change who he is; he just upgrades the tools. That's what I've been chasing: not fame, but amplification. This book is my Iron Man suit. My way of turning every scar, story, and slightly traumatizing life lesson into something that serves more people than it hurts.

But my acting origin story didn't begin under the Hollywood sign—it started in Toledo, Ohio, not exactly a known hub for cinematic greatness. I was in my second year of college when my friend Ben invited me to check out his church, Cedar Creek. As a Catholic kid, I was trained to associate church with hymnals, incense, and messages so dry they could double as desiccant packets. We called falling asleep mid-mass "Nicene Creed Napping."

Imagine my shock, then, when I walked into Cedar Creek and thought I'd entered a Christian Coachella. There was a full band. People were talking. Loudly. Some were even *cheering*. And the biggest miracle of all: there were *people my age*. I thought, *There's a chance I could meet someone here.* Then service started, and instead of a priest, there was a *cast*. On a *set*. Performing *skits*. I looked around thinking, *Is this God-legal?*

Cedar Creek changed everything I thought I'd known about faith and creativity. It loosened the guilt I'd carried since childhood, that quiet Catholic shame that says if you're having fun, you're probably doing it wrong. It also unlocked a creative side of me I didn't know existed. Cedar Creek was where I met Casey, the drama director, who became my acting coach *and* my spiritual hype woman. Under her guidance, I performed skits during services, little three-minute parables where I could make people laugh, think, or cry (sometimes all three). That was when I realized God was using performance to prep me for purpose. Cedar Creek was my proving ground: Toledo's version of Hollywood, but with less Botox and more baptism.

I lost touch with Casey and Ben over the years, but I'll never forget what they built into me. Casey's light sparked my creative confidence, and Ben? He's now the lead pastor of that same church. Not even Iron Man could've pulled off that kind of character arc.

How I Met My Guy Joe

Two years into L.A., and things were going exactly as you'd expect for a new actor: not great. I was praying for a divine plot twist or at least a commercial gig that would pay in something other than "exposure." Enter 24-Hour Fitness, Sherman Oaks. That's apparently the unspoken set of every C-list celebrity's workout montage. I lived three minutes away, which made it convenient for both bicep curls and identity crises. I'd also started offering personal training on the side to make rent, but what I didn't know was that this particular gym was *the* celebrity watering hole. I'd see everyone from TV stars there to people whose IMDb credits I had to google under "Are they still working?"

One day, mid-set, I noticed a guy lifting weights with a Terrible Towel. Steelers merch. My people! God bless my dad for raising me a Steelers fan in Browns territory. That's not fandom, that's faith. I looked closer and thought, *That's the guy from* How I Met Your Mother.

So, I walked up, introduced myself, told him I was a fan of the show, and, *BOOM!* I found myself talking to Joe Manganiello. And not just a quick handshake—we were having a real conversation. He's humble, hilarious, and nothing like the Hollywood stereotype.

Now, timing isn't always my spiritual gift. I'm bold, but sometimes my "Go for it!" energy doesn't check in with "Should I?" first. Still, I took my shot: "If you ever want to train, I'm a personal trainer." And get this—he said yes.

Next thing I knew, I was training *Joe Manganiello*. Eventually, the business part faded and the friendship took over. He became my closest friend in Los Angeles. Possibly my *only* friend at the time, but let's not focus on that.

Joe opened doors I hadn't even known existed. One night, he invited me out for dinner with "some guys." I was thinking Buffalo Wild Wings and football. I walked in, and the first person I saw was *Arnold Schwarzenegger*. Yes, *the* Terminator. The man whose biceps built entire genres. When I was introduced to him, I don't remember what I said, but I'm 90% sure it was not in English. Meeting him was like shaking hands with Mount Olympus. We took a group photo, proof that God occasionally answers oddly specific prayers.

That dinner led to more surreal nights and life lessons. Joe has had the kind of career most people can only dream about, yet he has stayed grounded, generous, and genuinely kind. Without chasing acting, I'd have never met him, and honestly, that friendship was worth every rejection, every audition flop, every unpaid gig. Sometimes the reward for pursuing your dream isn't the dream, it's who you meet along the way.

Anita and P.F. Chang's

Cut to me working at P.F. Chang's, slinging lettuce wraps and unsolicited life advice for tips. Entry-level pay at SoCalGas didn't stretch very far, so I was moonlighting as a server/bartender/stand-up comic. My strategy: if I could make customers laugh, my shift would feel shorter and maybe my tip jar would be fuller.

One night, a woman at my table laughed, but not the normal kind, more like she was mid-epiphany. She stopped me *mid-joke* (a violation punishable by eternal side-eye) and asked, "What do you want to do with your life?"

Ma'am. I'm holding a tray of dumplings. This is not the time for an existential ambush. But I answered honestly: "I want to be an actor."

She smirked. "Yeah, you and five million other people in L.A. But what do you *really* want to do?"

Something about the way she said it—calm, piercing, Holy Spirit-ish—hit me in the gut. Between the caffeine, Mongolian beef, and God's timing, I blurted out, "I want to help people realize they're more than they think they are."

She smiled, handed me a business card, and said, "Then that's what we're gonna do."

We? I looked at the card. It said "Talent Manager."

Cue angel choir. Cue disbelief. Cue me quoting Eminem: "If you had one shot or one opportunity / To seize everything you ever wanted in one moment / Would you capture it or just let it slip?"

It was one of those divine intersections where psychology meets providence, the exact moment when faith and serendipity hold hands. Anita became my manager and my encourager. Within weeks, I was auditioning for real shows, real films, real rooms where my name was spelled correctly on a call sheet. Each audition was a new exercise in humility and self-belief. I learned that faith isn't about getting *every* role, it's about trusting that the right ones won't miss you.

The Greek

Random Tuesday. Sunny Sherman Oaks. Birds chirping, rent due, dreams intact. Then my phone rang and it was Anita. Not just *any* call. THE call. "I got you a gig," she said.

I froze. "A gig as in...someone's going to *pay* me to act? Like real money? Not exposure or free coffee?"

"Yep. You're booked for background work on a new movie called *Get Him to the Greek*. You're on set at 6 a.m. tomorrow."

6 a.m. The time of day God invented for farmers and regret. But this was it: my shot. I was finally joining the cinematic elite...as "Guy Standing Behind Other Guy #7."

BTW, a quick aside about the acting world. In order to work on real movies and TV shows, you need to have your SAG card (Screen Actors Guild, the Hollywood union that protects actors from being paid in pizza and promises). But in order to get your SAG card, you have to be working on real movies and TV shows. This is why it takes a lifetime to be an overnight success. "Background work" is code for "You're technically in the movie, but only your mom will notice." Still, it matters. If you land three SAG background credits, you become SAG-Eligible. That's the velvet rope of the acting world; it's like getting an invitation to the Oscars of opportunity.

So, I drove to the address Anita gave me. It looked sketchier than a gas station sushi bar: back alley, no signage, just a metal door and a single light bulb flickering like it was in a horror movie.

I knocked. A literal mountain opened the door. "What are you here for?" he growled.

Existentially or professionally? was what I thought. But what came out was, "Background casting."

He pointed me inside.

I walked in and immediately realized this was not a normal film set—there were topless women walking around like it was Bring Your Trauma to Work Day. Turned out, I'd wandered into a strip club. My inner Catholic was already trying to light a candle. My first thought was, *What kind of movie is this?* My second thought was, *What kind of talent manager do I have?*

I checked in and confirmed: it was indeed *Get Him to the Greek,* not *Get Him to the Freak (Off).* For the next eight hours, my job was to walk behind a scene with a woman, pretending we were heading to the champagne room. Which, honestly, was a convincing bit of acting because I had no idea where the champagne room even was. Then I heard a voice shout, "Hey, tall guy in the back!"

It was Judd Apatow. *The* Judd Apatow.

When you're 6'2", "tall guy in the back" can only mean one thing: divine promotion.

"Come sit up front," he said.

I wanted to sprint up there before he changed his mind, but I was worried I'd trip and emotionally die in a strip club. So, I walked. Calmly. Casually. Like my knees weren't negotiating with gravity. And now, seated in behind me: Jonah Hill. Russell Brand. And one other actor we won't name because, well...Google is your friend.

Apatow yelled, "Action!"

Music blared. Out walked a *completely naked woman* who proceeded to perform an interpretive dance directly in front of me. Meanwhile, the stars were behind me, meaning the camera was pointed *at me.* My brain went into emergency prayer mode: *Dear Lord, I know You see me right now. Please focus the camera on my soul.*

When the movie came out months later, I hosted a personal red-carpet screening with an audience of three: Joe, Anita, and my therapist. And there it was: zero point three glorious seconds of screen time. Dead center.

It wasn't an Oscar moment. But it was proof that persistence pays off. That proximity creates opportunity. That God can use *any* set, even a strip club, to remind you He's not done writing your story. Psychologists call this the peak-end rule—we remember the moments when our emotions peaked or signaled the ending of a chapter. For me, that fleeting frame wasn't just a peak. It was a promise.

I'd go on to land two more background gigs and become SAG-Eligible. One foot in the dream! But right when I thought I'd reached the edge of breakthrough, God rerouted my GPS. He started whispering new dreams, ones that didn't involve memorizing lines but changing lives. I was growing at SoCalGas, mentoring people, solving problems, and realizing my leadership roles were another kind of stage. I didn't need a camera to perform; I needed purpose.

So, I doubled down. Got my Professional Engineer's license in thermal fluid systems (which sounds like something Iron Man would major in). Then I got an MBA from USC (cardinal and gold...also very Iron Man-esque). Each step pulled me deeper into influence and further away from acting. By the time I looked up, six years had passed. No big goodbye to the acting dream. Just a quiet fade-out, like a scene that ends before the credits roll.

But here's what I've realized: every seed God plants grows into something, even if it's not what you expected. That creative spark I found at Cedar Creek? It never died. It just evolved. Acting got me to L.A. It introduced me to Joe. It stretched my faith, my confidence, and my ability to connect with anyone. It taught me empathy, timing, and emotional intelligence, all things psychologists say define great leaders. Turns out, God wasn't training me to perform. He was training me to *communicate.*

So maybe my acting career didn't end—maybe it pivoted. Because what is leadership, really, if not a live performance of faith, courage, and grace under pressure? Is the acting dream finished? Maybe. Or maybe it's just intermission. God's the director and I'm just keeping my mark, staying in frame, waiting for the next cue. Until then, I'll keep taking stages, testing scripts, and living scenes that feel bigger than me. Because I've seen enough to know that when God's producing your story, everything truly is within reach.

Callings Never Stop

The thing about callings is that they don't expire—they just evolve. You think you've reached the credits, but then God just adds a post-credit scene. That chapter of my life taught me that purpose doesn't always arrive in the package you prayed for. Sometimes it's wrapped in failure, friendship, or a film set that smells vaguely like bad decisions and popcorn. But every one of those moments is a rehearsal for what comes next. The real art isn't in arriving, it's in refusing to believe you're done.

CHAPTER 19

The Subtle Discipline of Showing Up One More Time

There's a strange calm that comes after a dream dies. It's not peace, exactly—it's more like the quiet hum after fireworks, when the smoke's still in the air and you're trying to figure out if what just happened was beautiful or catastrophic. That's where I found myself: somewhere between "It's over!" and "What now?"

I used to think progress was a straight line: you start, you grind, you win. But life, faith, and a few humbling detours taught me that life is more like a loop. You circle back to lessons you swore you'd already mastered, people you thought you'd outgrown, and dreams you thought you'd buried. If you listen closely, you can hear God whispering the same three words every time: "Not done yet."

This kind of post-traumatic growth is the transformation that happens *through* pain, not despite it. It's redemption, the divine recycling program where nothing you lived through goes to waste. Grace doesn't always mean "Go!"—sometimes it means "Grow."

The Myth of the Finish Line and Finishing "Strong"

I'll confess that I've quit more things than I've finished. Maybe you have, too. Half-read books. Half-started gym routines. Half-eaten salads. Every motivational quote told me to "Never give up!" Meanwhile, my attention span said, "Counterpoint: we could."

We live in a world obsessed with finish lines, diplomas, promotions, weddings, retirements, and those "We made it!" posts with suspiciously perfect lighting. It's like life has become one big ceremony where we're supposed to smile like we've reached enlightenment just because we crossed some imaginary finish line. But life's not a marathon, it's a chaotic group project where half the team dropped out, the other half's winning, and someone's still trying to find the Google Doc link.

And yet, somehow we show up. We crawl. We improvise. We pray. We try again. That's the subtle art of *not done yet.* It's not glamorous and it rarely trends. But it's the quiet reason why the people who keep showing up—even they're limping—eventually lap everyone who looked like they had it all figured out.

Finish lines are addictive because they trick your brain into thinking, *This is where meaning lives.* But neuroscience tells a different story: our brains are wired to crave *progress*, not perfection. Dopamine fires during pursuit, not completion. It's like Heaven's little nudge that says, "Keep moving! I'm not done teaching you yet." Maybe we've been celebrating the wrong thing—maybe the real flex isn't crossing the line, it's having the faith to admit, "I'm still in the race."

Speaking of that finish line, "Finish strong" sounds noble until you realize no one ever tells you what to do in the middle. The middle is where dreams go to die or be resurrected, depending on your caffeine intake and prayer life. The gym's packed in January and a ghost town by March. That "new business idea" feels like destiny for two weeks and a bad decision by Week 6. The playlist repeats, the motivation fades, and your brain starts whispering, "Maybe this isn't for us..."

Nobody throws parades for persistence, but the middle is where identity happens. This liminal space is the in-between state where transformation actually roots itself. It's the cocoon stage. Messy. Isolating. Necessary. Faith calls it the *wilderness.* The Israelites spent forty years there, not because God lost the GPS signal, but because transformation takes time. The middle rewires you even though nobody likes the middle. It's the puberty of progress: everything's changing, nothing fits, and your faith's voice keeps cracking. You're too far from who you were and not yet who you're becoming. To be blunt, you're in emotional limbo.

This middle phase is also when neural pruning happens—your brain is deleting old habits to make room for better ones. So, if you're in that in-between where you feel lost, confused, or allergic to optimism, congratulations! You're not broken, you're buffering, and buffering is progress in disguise. You're quietly becoming the kind of person who can finish *anything.*

Grit Isn't Loud

People think grit sounds like a motivational scream in a cold shower. Nah... That's caffeine and unresolved childhood trauma. Real grit is quiet. It's showing up to the meeting where no one listens. It's writing another page that no one reads (yet). It's trusting God's plan when He's gone radio silent for three business quarters.

Psychologically, grit activates your anterior cingulate cortex, the brain's "Keep going!" switch. The more you push through discomfort, the less your brain panics the next time. Spiritually, it's the same principle: every act of persistence is a prayer in motion. You're telling Heaven, "I still believe this is worth it."

Grit doesn't say, "I got this." It whispers, "I'll try again tomorrow." And that whisper, repeated enough times, turns into unshakable belief and a willingness to push past the 90%. That's where it's horrifically tempting to quit, not out of a sense of laziness but because 90% *feels* like "almost done." It's not, though—it's actually closer to the halfway point. It's also where the real test begins.

When the novelty's gone and your brain starts throwing tantrums like a toddler denied snacks, that's when motivation dies and identity has to take over. That 90% is a testing ground: when you've trained your brain and your faith to connect effort with self-respect, you stop needing applause. You stop finishing for validation. Instead, you finish because quitting doesn't fit your spiritual DNA anymore. That's identity-based grit: "I don't finish because it's fun. I finish because it's who I am now."

Dopamine, that mischievous little neurotransmitter, doesn't reward *achievement,* it rewards *pursuit.* That's why you feel high chasing the goal and oddly empty after achieving it. You think God's being silent? Maybe He's just stretching your dopamine tolerance. Teaching you that fulfillment is in *movement,* not milestones.

In short, persistence isn't willpower—it's chemistry + calling. Every "I kept going" moment literally rewires your brain and strengthens your faith muscle. Grit is one more prayer, one more email, one more "Lord, give me strength before I send this text." Each repetition becomes a neurological *and* a spiritual receipt that says "Progress is the point."

Of course, we all have that season where we whisper, "I can't do this anymore." And God whispers back, "Then you're probably close." That "almost broke me" era feels like a deleted scene from a coming-of-age movie: ugly crying in your car, trying to pray while Spotify ads interrupt with offers for car insurance. But that moment is friction, not failure, and friction creates fire.

One client I coached applied to sixty-three jobs. Got ghosted more times than a bad Tinder date. After eight months, she was done, at least until she had one last why-not? interview. That became her dream job. Not because she got lucky, but because she was *still standing there* when her opportunity showed up. That's the cruel math of faith and grit: you don't get to pick when the miracle lands, but you *do* get to decide whether you're still in the room when it does.

Failure's PR Problem

Failure's been getting bad press for centuries. If it had Yelp reviews, it would read "1 star. Made me cry in public." But failure's not the villain! It's just the unpaid intern of growth being underappreciated and over-worked while constantly trying to clean up our messes. Failure's job isn't to destroy us, it's to delete the version of us that can't handle what's next.

Psychologically, failure triggers our default-mode network, the intro-spection zone that lights up when we reflect or replay every awkward thing we've ever done. Spiritually, that's the same system God uses to upgrade our perspective. So yeah, failure hurts. But so does leg day, and we still pretend *that's* fine.

Grit means crying *strategically*, like when you scream-pray in your car and then walk into the meeting like, "We're good." That's not delusion, that's sanctified resilience. But of course, there's a thin line between grit and grind, and most of us have tripped over it face-first at some point. Perseverance is courageous. Stubbornness is caffeine-flavored denial. Or if you want to put it in psychological terms, it's called cognitive entrench-ment, the brain's polite way of saying, "We've invested too much for our ego to admit that we're wrong."

Real perseverance asks, "Is this still serving who I'm becoming?" Stubbornness asks, "How *dare* reality disrespect my plan?" Sometimes *not done yet* means pivoting, not pushing. Quitting a dead path is emotional refinancing—you're freeing up energy for something that'll actually pay eternal dividends.

Everyone loves the *idea* of grit until they realize it's repetitive, boring, and deeply unphotogenic, but that's where transformation hides: in the unposted moments. *Not done yet* is a lifestyle, a sacred address somewhere between "almost there" and "God's not finished."

You don't need to be the fastest. You don't need to be the strongest. You just need to refuse to label "unfinished" as failure. The best people you'll ever meet are all still under construction: tired, imperfect, hilarious works in progress. That's evolution + grace in real time.

The Value of Humor and Micro-Grit

The most underrated survival skill on earth is comedy. Life is a sitcom with no script supervisor, and if you can't laugh, you'll drown in dramatic irony. Humor is your nervous system saying, "We're safe enough to joke now." Laughter is a parasympathetic reset—it lowers cortisol, boosts endorphins, and convinces your body you're not in danger. So yeah, sometimes the holiest thing you can do mid-meltdown is narrate your crisis like David Attenborough: "And here we observe the adult human, attempting to assemble their life with only coffee and optimism…"

Grit without humor becomes martyrdom. Grit *with* humor becomes resilience with a wink, the kind Heaven high-fives you for, the kind that lets you foster micro-grit every day. Micro-grit is brushing your teeth and your ego even after rejection and opening the laptop when your soul's on low battery. This aggregation of marginal gains—small, repeated improvements that compound—builds micro-grit into solid, long-lasting, lifelong grit.

To have more micro-grit in your life, try the five-minute rule: do the hard thing for five minutes. Once you start, dopamine releases for progress, not perfection. Spiritually, that's momentum meeting mercy. Micro-grit doesn't post on social media, it builds character in silence. And *that's* where greatness and grace quietly grow. That's also where you can gain the fortitude you need to kick out perfectionism, a.k.a. grit's evil twin, the one that catches you in a self-worth contingency trap where your value depends on flawless execution.

Micro-grit gives you the perspective to see that "done enough" isn't laziness, it's liberation. The people who wait for perfect never release the thing, while the people who embrace "done enough" build empires out of awkward first drafts and holy exhaustion. So, tell your inner critic, "You're not the boss of dopamine!" And then hit Send.

WITHIN REACH TOOLKIT
The Grit Grid™

Here's the formula algebra forgot: **Progress = (Tiny Wins ÷ Time) × Belief.** Momentum + delusional faith will net you micro-wins, and each one of those will compound like emotional interest. One morning, you'll wake up inside a life that used to feel impossible. Psychologically, that's hedonic elevation: sustained micro-joy builds durable happiness. Spiritually, it's faith muscle memory.

Progress isn't heroic, it's statistical—keep trying long enough, and the odds will eventually surrender. Progress also does *not* equal grind! You can't "hustle" your way through exhaustion. Sometimes grit means taking a nap with conviction. Rest is a much-needed Sabbath, and *everybody* needs it—according to the recovery paradox, the harder you work, the more strategic rest you need.

Burnout doesn't come from doing too much, it comes from doing too much without meaning or margin. Resilience without rest becomes resentment. So, take the nap or watch something dumb. And then rise again. With grit. Here are some easy ways to develop more of it:

Step 1: The three-minute audit.

Ask yourself:

- What did I almost quit today?
- Why didn't I?
- What did that teach me about who I'm becoming?

Write it down. Some might call this journaling; some might call it emotional bookkeeping for Heaven's accountants.

Step 2: The 1% rule.

Forget giant leaps! Go for 1% increments by asking yourself, "What's one tiny act of obedience I can do today?"

Step 3: The still-standing score.

Rate yourself on a scale of 1 to 10 on how often you showed up despite not feeling like it. If your numbers are inching up, you're compounding grit and faith.

Step 4: The done-enough declaration.

Say it aloud (bonus points if people stare): "I'm not done yet, but I'm proud of how far God's brought me."

That rewires your brain to connect effort with pride instead of exhaustion.

Step 5: The refuel ritual.

Once a week, do something that restores your soul, not your résumé. Laugh. Breathe. Nap like it's a meeting you can't cancel. Because no grit survives without grace.

When "Not Yet" Becomes "Now"

The thing about waiting seasons is that they don't announce when they're over—you just wake up one day and realize the delay you resented was actually direction in disguise. That every detour, every "almost," every door that didn't open was quietly rerouting you toward the one that finally would. Learning to trust the unseen edits is the subtle art of not being done. Because while you're pacing, praying, and wondering if you missed your cue, God's backstage, rewriting the scene so the timing makes sense later. It's pattern recognition in action—our brain's way of connecting dots in hindsight. Faith calls it providence, the moment you realize those dots were divine all along.

And then it happens: that Monday night, that unexpected email, that sudden opportunity, that holy plot twist that makes you laugh and cry because it feels like Heaven just said, "See? I told you we weren't done." Suddenly, everything you had thought about yourself and where you were heading gets flipped with one single word.

CHAPTER 20

The Monday Night Plot Twist I Never Saw Coming

You never think the night your life changes will start with a stale buffet roll and a name badge that won't stick. It was a Monday, the most aggressively average day of the week, in Omaha, Nebraska, of all places. I wasn't chasing destiny, I was chasing decaf. But that's the thing about God: He hides holy moments in painfully ordinary settings.

The ballroom lights buzzed like tired angels, the air smelled like corporate ambition and carpet cleaner, and somewhere between my second coffee and third self-doubt spiral, I felt it—that internal tug that says, "Something's coming." It felt like the quiet kind of weight that settles before Heaven turns a page. It was liminality, the in-between space where one version of you is fading and another is about to begin. Unbeknownst to me, I had walked into a collision between fear, purpose, and the God Who apparently has a flair for dramatic timing.

The Voice That Wouldn't Shut Up

Okay, I'll just get this out of the way: yes, I hear voices. But before you call HR or a pastor, let me clarify that it's just *one* voice, the same voice that's been squatting rent-free in my brain since middle school. While other kids had "Eye of the Tiger" as their inner anthem, mine was more like "Acoustic Sadness: Volume Infinite." The chorus kept singing, "You're not enough." Catchy, right? It's a Billboard Top 10 on the Overthinkers' Hot 100 list.

That voice played everywhere: school, job interviews, first dates, even during small talk with baristas. Somewhere along the way, it stopped being background noise and became my narrator. British accent optional; judgmental tone guaranteed. It never screamed, which is exactly how self-doubt works—rather than shouting, "You're worthless!", it politely suggests, "You're not built for this." If my brain had Yelp reviews, that voice would have five stars for persistence and zero for customer service.

Despite that constant soundtrack, though, I managed to convince a shocking number of people that I had it all together. Career growing? Check. Team leading? Check. Pretending not to spiral during performance reviews? Check, with confetti. I was the PowerPoint version of a functioning adult: lots of transitions, questionable content, decent font choice.

By early 2024, I'd made peace with the idea that "almost but not quite enough" was my destiny. My tombstone was basically pre-engraved: *Here lies John. Almost impressive and almost memorable...* Then came Omaha and that fateful Monday.

I was there because my company had announced auditions to host our semi-annual conference that would consist of 700 people, among them executives and our CEO. Basically, all of our corporate Avengers would be present. This was my shot! After all, I was a former actor and an extrovert (who maybe had the attention span of a goldfish at a fireworks show). So, I walked in with the confidence of someone who just discovered caffeine and purpose at the same time.

I crushed it! I knew I had gotten the gig! ...Except I didn't. Three engineers—people who literally say "tensile strength" for fun—had somehow outperformed the ex-actor. That's the equivalent of losing in *The Voice* to someone who only does sign language. But grace has a sense of humor, and in this case, that grace was given human form by people who said, "John, we'd still love for you to host the entertainment portion of Monday night..."

Before they had even finished the sentence, I yelled, "YES!!" Classic me, committing faster than my anxiety could object. Somewhere in Heaven, God probably whispered, "He said yes... He has no idea what's coming."

Fast-forward a few months. I had written a fifteen-minute monologue that was supposed to blend *Jimmy Kimmel Live!* and our unique corporate lingo perfectly. Then came rehearsal. And I tanked. Spectacularly. No one laughed *with* me unless you count the pity laughs after many awkward moments of silence. Lines vanished, pacing collapsed, confidence went missing and is still probably listed as "unclaimed baggage" somewhere in Nebraska.

Cue the voice: "You're not enough." My brain offered immediate exit strategies:

1. Pretend you lost your voice.
2. Claim COVID.
3. Move to Canada and start a maple syrup testimony tour.

That's the thing about fear—it's wildly creative when you give it the mic.

After the pity claps, I did what every overthinker with unresolved perfectionism does: I overcompensated. I locked myself into my hotel room and rehearsed until my neurons were able to file a union grievance. I practiced so long I started answering myself in applause breaks. By Monday night, I was ready. Or at least, I told myself I was.

Then, minutes before walking on stage, the voice came back. Louder. Meaner. "You're not enough. And you know it!" And this time, my body listened: my throat tightened, my heart rate spiked, and my vision tunneled. My nervous system went full fight-flight-or-faint.

They cued me to walk up... and I didn't. For two eternal seconds, I just stood there, frozen like a Windows update at 99%. Seven hundred people staring. Lights hot. Air thick. My inner monologue promptly told me, "This is when they figure out you're a fraud." But then something shifted. Not theatrically—spiritually. It was as if God Himself gave me a slight nudge. And for the first time in my adult life, the voice went silent. Then, in the quiet that followed, another voice—calm, amused, unmistakably divine—whispered: "You can do this. You're not *doing* enough."

Wait. What? Did God just edit my anxiety? At first, I thought I'd misheard. But deep down, I knew: that wasn't condemnation, it was a calling. Maybe I'd been misinterpreting the whole soundtrack of my life. Maybe the voice wasn't saying I *wasn't enough*, maybe it had been reminding me I'd been *underusing* what He'd already given me.

I took a step. Then another. My body moved before my brain caught up. I started talking. They started laughing. I remembered my lines. Nobody left.

Obviously, there's a one-word difference between "You're not enough" and "You're not *doing* enough." But that one word is everything. The first freezes you in shame; the second fires you into action. The realization hit me mid-laughter, mid-lights, mid-life: God wasn't trying to fix my confidence, He was trying to activate my stewardship. Because faith isn't thinking you *have* enough, it's trusting that God *is* enough and that He gave you what you need to start. Which is why that Monday night didn't just change my career, it rewired my identity.

WITHIN REACH TOOLKIT
The Voice Shift Framework

Here's your own version of a Monday night that you can practice without having to go through the stage fright.

Step 1: Catch the voice.

Write down the recurring phrase that hijacks your thoughts. (Example: "You're not enough.") You can't mute what you don't first identify! If you ignore it, that phrase will start narrating your life like it's a sad documentary. Don't let it do that.

Step 2: Change the script.

When you change the script from "You're not enough" to "You're not doing enough with what you've been given," that rewires your self-talk from *identity* to *action*. It's not who you are, it's *what you're capable of expanding into.*

Step 3: Clarify the call.

Ask yourself, "What am I being nudged to do more of?" Courage? Consistency? Kindness? Forgiveness? Write down one small, specific step you can take to go in that direction. Movement beats magnitude every time.

Step 4: Create the counter-voice.

Replace the lie with truth. Record yourself saying: "You have everything you need." "You're built for this." "This isn't failure, it's feedback." Listen daily until your own voice sounds like faith.

Step 5: Condition the loop.

Repeat the new truth until your neurons surrender to it. Repetition builds belief; belief builds evidence; evidence builds peace. That's not manifesting, that's neuroplasticity baptized in grace.

When you think "I'm not enough," your amygdala—the brain's fear alarm—lights up like a siren. It floods your system with cortisol, convincing your body to panic. But when you shift to "I'm not doing enough," then your prefrontal cortex takes the mic. That's your logic and action hub. It calms the fear response and opens the door to problem-solving. That's how God designed you: the same brain chemistry that fuels fear can also fuel faith, depending on which words you choose to believe.

Language doesn't just describe your reality, it designs it. Shame says, "I'm broken." Stewardship says, "I've got more to give." The goal is to upgrade the voice's vocabulary. Because sometimes God doesn't quiet the storm in your head, He just teaches you to hear it differently. Once you start listening to the voice with curiosity instead of criticism—once you stop seeing it as an enemy and start seeing it as a teacher—you'll realize it was never saying "You're not enough." It was whispering, "You're not done yet."

Quick Ways to Reframe the Voice

NEGATIVE VOICE	EMPOWERED TRANSLATION
"You're not enough."	"You're not doing enough with what you've got."
"You're falling behind."	"You're being called forward."
"You failed."	"You just learned faster than most."
"You're stuck."	"You're stabilizing before your next leap."

When the Applause Fades but the Echo Stays

When the ballroom emptied that night, I didn't feel victorious, I felt exposed. It's weird how Breakthrough and Vulnerability show up holding hands. Everyone else heard a talk, but I heard a wake-up call I couldn't unhear. Once you've had a moment like that—one when God rewrites your fear in front of an audience—you don't just go back to normal. You go back to war...with your own head.

Suddenly, it's just you and that familiar internal voice, the one that's been narrating your insecurities since middle school. Only now, you can't ignore it—you start noticing its tone, its timing, its PR strategy, the way it spins half-truths into headlines. You realize that the voice in your head just needs a rebrand. In other words, that voice needs stewardship—you need to learn to take the mic back and remind your mind who's *really* running the show.

CHAPTER 21

Why Your Thoughts Lie and How to Rewrite the Script

After that Monday night, the same voice that used to whisper, "You're not enough" started trying out new material: "You're not doing enough," "You're falling behind," "Maybe God picked the wrong person." But the truth is, the voice in my head wasn't evil, it was just misinformed. It had bad PR. It didn't know how to speak the language of peace yet.

Psychologists call that voice our inner narrator. It's a running commentary of our life that can either amplify our potential or sabotage it. Faith calls it spiritual static, the interference that keeps us from hearing the frequency of grace clearly. And I call it... Tuesday.

The Noisy Room Between Your Ears

Let's be honest: your brain isn't a temple, it's a group chat with bad Wi-Fi. One friend's overanalyzing that text you sent in 2012. Another's doomscrolling through imaginary worst-case scenarios. And there's always one who shows up at 3 a.m. saying something like, "Hey, remember that embarrassing thing you said in fourth grade?" Sometimes the inner DJ plays a hit, that "I got this!" anthem before a presentation. But most days, the album is more *Lo-Fi Anxious Beats to Study Your Failures To*. Plot twist: all of those characters are you.

You can't silence the noise. Nobody can. You *can*, however, become the producer of your ever-present inner stage play. Pick the tracks. Remix the narrative. Fade out the fear before it drops the next verse. Peace is learning how to run sound check with grace. And when the static gets loud, remember: God doesn't shout over your chaos, He speaks *through* it. You just have to stop scrolling long enough to hear Him say, "Hey... I'm still here."

Every human I've met—CEOs, students, baristas—seems to believe the same "I'll be at peace when..." myth. "When I finally get the job." "When I finally lose the weight." "When my parents finally say they're proud." We all participate in the arrival fallacy, the lie that tells us that happiness exists just one little accomplishment away. Faith calls it what it is: the idolatry of "next." Because every time you say, "I'll rest when I achieve X," you're accidentally worshiping the goal instead of the Giver.

Science agrees that this kind of self-misdirection is foolish, because your brain is going to move the goalpost as soon as you reach it. (Thank you, hedonic treadmill.) You hit one milestone, and forty-eight hours later, the voice whispers, "Cool! Now do it again." But you can't negotiate peace, you can only *practice* it. And contrary to popular belief, real peace isn't noise-*canceling*, it's noise-*organizing*. Peace is reading a stressful text and not emotionally detonating. Peace is knowing that chaos doesn't mean God left the chat.

Your nervous system's an orchestra and peace is the conductor. Without it, your thoughts just create an angry cacophony in the background; *with it*, your values, goals, and grace get into rhythm and even the noise becomes music. That's why the most peaceful people you know aren't calm, they're *clarified*. They didn't wait for stillness—they rehearsed perspective until it became muscle memory. They turned panic into prayer and fear into focus.

When you find your thoughts start to circle like seagulls at a picnic, you can do a quick mental reset by asking yourself these questions:

1. What tone am I using with myself right now?
2. Would I speak to someone I love this way?
3. What emotion am I feeding with this thought?
4. How can I reframe this as gratitude?
5. What story would the calm version of me tell right now?

Bonus: What would this same scenario look like on mute? If I couldn't narrate it, how bad would it really be?

Five (okay, six) questions. One reset. Think of it like prayer with a clipboard: reflection plus self-regulation.

Why Positive Self-Talk Works (But Not the Cringe Kind)

We all love affirmations…until they start sounding like they were written by a motivational raccoon: "I am a radiant beam of infinite power." The problem with toxic positivity is that your brain isn't dumb. If you tell yourself "I'm amazing!" while your soul's screaming "I'm exhausted!", your prefrontal cortex marks it as spam.

The fix? Accurate optimism. Not denial, redirection. Psychologists call it cognitive reframing. Faith calls it renewing your mind.

Try this:

- Instead of saying "I'm not ready," say, "I'm learning fast."
- Instead of "I'm broken," say, "I'm under renovation."
- Instead of "I'm behind," say, "I'm on God's schedule."

Every reframe is emotional aikido—you're using the weight of your worry against itself. Do that enough, and you're not lying to yourself, you're aligning with the truth. I saw this principle in action when I knew a guy named Bobby. His thoughts were like bad coworkers: always late, always negative, and always calling "urgent" meetings when situations could've been handled with a simple email. He'd crush a project and his inner voice would say, "That was luck." He'd get praise. His voice would tell him, "They're just being polite." He'd post on LinkedIn. Voice: "Wow, everyone probably hates this."

Finally, his therapist dropped a line that deserved its own sermon slide: "Try talking to yourself the way you'd talk to someone you love."

Bobby laughed. "If my best friend talked to me the way *I* talk to me, I'd block him." That was when it hit him: he didn't have a confidence problem, he had a *customer service* problem with his own thoughts. So, he started writing to his brain like he was running a support desk.

Thought: "You're not smart enough." Brian: "That's cute. You said that last time. I crushed it." Thought: "You'll probably fail." Brian: "Maybe. But failure has better character development than quitting." The more he practiced compassionate accuracy, the more his brain learned a new language: truth. That's neuroplasticity, baby! Repetition builds strength.

The Three Voices Inside You

Inside your head, there's a panel discussion going on with three participants:

The Critic: Snarky, judgmental, always armed with a microphone.

The Coach: Loud, passionate, occasionally unhinged.

The Calm One: Speaks once a week but drops wisdom like a monk with a latte.

Most people think they need to fire the Critic. Nope! The Critic's job is quality control—he just needs supervision. Without a bit of criticism, you'd post every half-baked idea you've ever had ("New side hustle: underwater candle store!"). The trick is to let the Coach translate and the Calm One moderate:

Critic: "You're not ready."

Coach: "Not yet, but we're training."

Calm One: "You've survived 100 % of your worst days so far. You'll survive this, too."

That's inner discipleship. God isn't calling you to silence the voices—you just need to let the right one lead the meeting. So, tomorrow morning, do something bold: look in the mirror and *listen*. Not to what you see, to what you *say*. You'll probably hear the Critic saying something like, "Woah, you look old!" Rarely do we look at ourselves and think, "Hey, look who's still showing up!" That's because self-talk is marketing, and most of us are running PR for our insecurities.

When you whisper, "I can't handle this," your subconscious turns it into a billboard; when you declare, "I'm terrible under pressure," that becomes your brand campaign. That's some pretty crappy marketing! Good thing you're ultimately the one in charge of it.

When I decided to up my PR game, I started testing my own branding. If the adjectives I used about myself wouldn't sound inspiring in someone else's LinkedIn bio, I rewrote them:

"I'm awkward" → **"I value authenticity."**

"I'm indecisive" → **"I think before I commit."**

"I'm stubborn" → **"I protect my boundaries."**

That's not spin, that's stewardship. *You* are the head of communications for your own potential, so *you* need to run better campaigns. When you catch yourself rehearsing failure in the mirror, remember that even Moses stuttered before he led. Moses actually tried to talk God out of using him—that's how terrified he was. But God knew exactly what He was doing with Moses, and He knows exactly what He is doing with you. God doesn't need you polished, just *present.*

I saw this transformation in action with Danielle. She was caffeine in human form: upbeat, kind, magnetic. Her team adored her. Clients praised her. She could hype everyone in the room...except herself. When she looked in the mirror, she didn't see what everyone else did. Her confidence, she realized, was like Wi-Fi: strong when connected to others, nonexistent when alone.

Then one morning, fed up with her own doubt, she tried something weird: verbal reps. One statement out loud every morning: "I've done hard things before." "I can figure this out." "I'm not behind, I'm becoming." At first, it felt cringe. Then awkward. Then *electric.*

By Week Three, her tone had shifted, her posture had changed, and her presence had expanded. (Her coworkers noticed all of this before she did.) She wasn't faking being confident because she had trained herself to actually *be* confident. This kind of embodied cognition happens when the act of speaking truth physically rewires the brain's self-belief. God's been telling us this ever since Genesis: "Speak, and it becomes."

Gratitude, too, has the power to move (internal) mountains. Take Marcus. He had everything: great salary, a Tesla, a forty-person team, and insomnia that could power Los Angeles. Every night, he'd rerun the "What Could Go Wrong?" marathon: he'd replay awkward pauses, double-check emails he'd already sent, and wonder if everyone secretly hated him. Then one night, delirious, he grabbed a notebook and wrote three things he'd done *right* that day:

- "Didn't interrupt Sarah."
- "Fixed the budget glitch."
- "Actually ate lunch."

The next night, he did the same thing. Then he did it again. Within two weeks, his brain started scanning for good things to *write down.* He'd woken up his reticular activating system, that part of the brain that filters what you notice. He was retraining it to search for progress, not problems. Gratitude was shifting his perception, not because life was getting easier, but because he was finally starting to count the right miracles.

By Week Four, Marcus was sleeping like someone who had finally turned off all his mental notifications.

The Subtle Flex: Self-Compassion Is a Power Move

Somewhere along the way, we confused self-compassion with weakness, as if being kind to ourselves meant we'd lose our edge. But grace doesn't dull ambition, it fuels endurance! When you mess up and choose empathy over judgment, you save energy, and energy is the currency of growth. Dr. Kristin Neff, author of *Mindful Self-Compassion for Burnout*, says, "Self-esteem is about how you compare to others. Self-compassion is about how you treat yourself when you don't."

That's not letting yourself off the hook, it's refusing to hang yourself on it. Even Jesus said, "Love your neighbor *as yourself*." Most of us skip the second half of that command. But it's not selfish to refill your cup, it's strategic to stop trying to pour from an empty one.

If your inner world's a war zone and self-compassion is nowhere to be found, no success will ever feel like victory—you'll outrun goals and still feel chased. But once your self-talk becomes intentional—not perfect, just *directed*—everything will change. Confidence will become a steady, quiet knowing, no performance needed. Peace will become proactive, not circumstantial. Success will stop feeling like a sprint and start feeling like a collaboration between who you are and who you're becoming.

So, the next time that voice in your head starts heckling, smile and say, "Thanks for the feedback, but the show has a new producer." Because it does. And spoiler: the Producer's name isn't fear anymore.

Your Thoughts' PR Department

If your brain were a company, your self-talk would be its marketing team, and if you're anything like me, that team should've been fired years ago. We've been out there running billboard campaigns for our flaws: "Now Hiring: Imposter Syndrome, Apply Within!" "Flash Sale on Self-Doubt, Everything Must Go (Including My Confidence)!" Time to hire new leadership.

Step 1: Audit the bad press.

List your five recurring "press releases." Maybe they're something like "I always mess up" or "I'm not creative" or "I don't belong here." Then ask yourself, "Would I publish this about someone I love?" If you wouldn't, congratulations! You just found fake news.

Step 2: Hire a better copywriter.

Your amygdala writes panic headlines. Your prefrontal cortex edits truth. Faith adds the tagline: "God's not done yet." So focus on the prefrontal cortex and turn "I'm behind" into "I'm pacing myself." Turn "I'm late" into "I'm on divine time."

Step 3: Redesign the messaging.

Create a three-line brand manifesto for your mental world:

1. Who I am: Not perfect, but progressing.
2. What I stand for: Curiosity, not comparison.
3. What I deliver: Consistency over chaos.

Print it. Say it. Pray it. Your brain listens to repetition more than it listens to reason.

Step 4: Manage your press releases.

When your inner critic runs in yelling, "Crisis! Someone on Twitter thinks you're a failure!", pause and smile. Say, "We'll issue a statement once the facts are verified." That's emotional regulation—or, as Grandma called it, wisdom.

Step 5: Track the metrics that matter.

Likes ≠ peace. Followers ≠ fulfillment. The new metrics are:

- How fast you recover.
- How kind you are under pressure.
- How much bandwidth you reclaim when you don't overthink everything.

That's ROIV: Return on Inner Voice.

Step 6: Launch the rebrand.

Your new slogan: "My thoughts don't define me, my responses do." Because real growth isn't having fewer negative thoughts, it's being *less convinced* by them. That's how you go from being your own worst critic to your own best publicist.

WITHIN REACH TOOLKIT
The R.A.D.I.O. Method™

Your mind's a radio station that never stops broadcasting, and if you don't grab the mic, static is going to take over. Enter R.A.D.I.O.: Rewiring Automatic Dialogue Into Optimism! Or where psychology meets peace and practice meets gospel calm.

Just practice rewiring one thought per day. Just *one*. Consistency, not volume, rewires defaults. Do it long enough, and your brain will start picking better background music: fewer panic anthems and more "God's still working on me" acoustic sets.

STEP	ACTION	EXAMPLE	WHY IT WORKS (PSYCHOLOGY + FAITH)
R: Recognize	Catch the thought before it catches you.	"Wait, who just said that in my head?"	Metacognition: Separates you from the thought. Awareness = first miracle.
A: Ask "Is it true?"	Challenge your internal headline.	"Would I say that to someone I love?"	Cognitive restructuring: Dismantles distortion. Truth always sets you free.
D: Detach from drama	Hit pause before spiraling.	"Will this matter in a week?"	Temporal distancing: Reduces cortisol; makes space for grace.
I: Inject a better question	Curiosity beats criticism.	"What can I learn from this?"	Neuroplasticity: Turns fear into data. Curiosity is holy courage.
O: Offer yourself the last word	Don't let anxiety close the show.	"I've done harder things and survived."	Self-compassion loop: Re-anchors safety. Faith adds: "Because God's still got me."

MINI TOOLKIT
"Rebrand Your Brain" Exercise

- Headline audit: Write down one recurring negative thought.
- Rewrite the press release: Turn it into language that's neutral or growth-based.
- Draft the quote: What would you tell a friend who was feeling this?
- Publish it: Repeat it aloud three times.

Old headline: "I'm not good at networking." New headline: "I'm learning how to connect more naturally." Quote: "Every conversation is a rep, and I'm getting stronger." That's taking discipleship of your dialogue.

And remember, the voice in your head isn't your enemy, it's your intern—your undertrained, overworked intern. It just needs better data, better direction, and a little divine grace. Because when your inner PR finally aligns with your God-given potential, the world won't just hear your voice speaking more loudly, it'll finally believe it.

When the Voice Goes Quiet but the Weight Remains

Once I stopped believing everything the voice in my head said, I thought I'd finally feel light again, but I found out that healing your mind doesn't always heal your habits. You can silence the critic and still keep carrying the armor, because even after the noise fades, the performance doesn't— you still walk into rooms trying to look composed, trying to prove you're okay, trying to lead while secretly limping. The voice might've been wrong about who I was, but it was right about one thing: I was *tired.*

Psychologists call that ego fatigue, the burnout that comes from managing the version of yourself you think everyone needs. Faith calls it weariness in well-doing. Either way, the armor that had once protected me started feeling like the very thing that was holding me back. I realized peace alone isn't enough—you have to learn to lay the armor down, too. Sometimes the bravest thing you can do is stop fighting battles God has already won.

CHAPTER 22

How God Uses Weight to Show You What Needs Letting Go

There comes a point when pretending to be strong starts to feel like cardio for your soul—you're smiling, grinding, and telling everybody, "I'm good!" while you're spiritually clutching a stress ball and googling "jobs that allow naps and purpose." You don't mean to wear the armor, you just forget to take it off. What started out as protection quietly became identity. Carrying turned into coping. Coping turned into character. Somewhere along the way, resilience became rebranding.

That's when rust creeps in. That armor gets heavy! It's the weight of every "I've got it" you said when you didn't. It's every time you prayed for strength and God whispered, "Or you could just rest." I thought faith was endurance, that the holier I was, the longer I could carry the load. But faith isn't about how long you can keep wearing armor, it's about how soon you can take it off.

I remember the day when my armor finally cracked. It was in a Chick-fil-A parking lot, because apparently God wanted to make sure there were waffle fries to comfort me. I'd just left a meeting where I'd smiled for an hour straight, nodding like a dashboard bobblehead that secretly hates every word being said.

I sat there in that parking lot gripping the steering wheel, eyes stinging, trying to remember if breathing was supposed to feel like buffering. Out loud, I whispered, "Man... This armor got heavy." It was a confession, maybe a spiritual one. Because sometimes the most faithful thing you can say isn't "I'm strong" but rather "I'm tired."

Armor Comes in Different Forms

Nobody warns us that adulthood comes with an emotional dress code that eventually turns into armor. As kids, we're emotionally naked: loud, honest, and unfiltered. Then somewhere between report cards and performance reviews, someone says, "Don't take things personally" and we start ironing our feelings. By our thirties, we've accessorized our soul. "Professionalism" becomes emotional shapewear: tight, polite, and just breathable enough to pass for composure. But deep down, everyone's craving permission to unzip a little and just say, "Honestly, I'm not okay, but I still love Jesus and I'm trying."

My personal brand of armor is executive calm. Picture serenity on the outside, internal screaming on the inside. I thought emotional neutrality was maturity. Turns out, it was just spiritual constipation.

See, your amygdala—that tiny almond-shaped alarm system in your brain—can't tell the difference between a bear in the woods and your boss saying, "Quick pivot!" Every time you sense rejection or failure, your brain goes DEFCON 1. So, you armor up. You flatten emotion. You turn faith into functionality. But every time you suppress vulnerability, your brain learns that emotion = danger. That's why staying stoic feels safe but slowly kills connection.

I once coached a manager named Carla. She was brilliant, polished, and untouchable. She could juggle eighteen projects but couldn't handle a genuine "How are you?" without saying "Busy, but good." Her team respected her but never related to her. But then one day, after a client meltdown, she finally admitted, "I'm scared we might lose this one."

And the wildest thing happened: nobody panicked. They exhaled. Her honesty didn't break her authority, it built it. Because people want leaders who are believable, not perfect. Armor earns applause; authenticity earns trust.

For me, humor has always been my favorite armor—I could hide pain inside punchlines like a magician hides doves up sleeves. "Oh, I'm not anxious," I'd joke. "I'm just preemptively caffeinated for tomorrow's problems."

Humor, when used right, is spiritual. It's grace in disguise, laughter that lightens the air long enough for truth to breathe. But used wrong, it's deflection with good timing. We deflect all the time, turning our pain into content before we've turned it into healing. But the joke hits differently when it's *not* a defense mechanism, when it's actually gratitude disguised as comedy. Sometimes the bravest thing you can do is let the joke land, pause before the punchline, and let the silence do its work. Laughter heals when it's honest.

Being Human—Being Vulnerable—Is Always the Right Choice

I once coached a CEO who had to announce layoffs. "I can't cry," he told me. "I have to stay strong."

"No," I said. "You absolutely should cry—you have to stay *human.*"

When it came time to announce the horrible news, halfway through his speech, his voice cracked. He paused, wiped his eyes, and said softly, "This is hard for me, too."

The room exhaled. They didn't need a hero, they needed a heartbeat to sync up with theirs. Neuroscience calls it limbic resonance; faith calls it compassion. Either way, when your nervous system syncs with someone else's, miracles happen. That day, the CEO didn't lose respect, he regained it. Because people follow authenticity, and vulnerability is at the heart of that.

The problem with vulnerability, though, is that even though everyone wants to make that kind of connection, nobody wants to go first. It's like emotional Wi-Fi: we're all waiting for someone else to turn it on. But you can't selectively numb feelings. When you mute sadness, you muffle joy. When you hide fear, you lose access to awe. When you armor up, you block both pain *and* purpose. We upgrade our armor and get a new job, a new house, and a new prayer journal, thinking that all of that will finally feel like peace. But fulfillment isn't a stronger signal, it's fewer walls.

If you trace your armor far enough back, you'll find the first incident that started it all. Maybe a teacher embarrassed you. Maybe a parent said, "Stop crying." You learned that *feeling equals punishment.* So, you built a wall. And over time, the guard became the warden. That's why you can look "successful" and still feel empty: safety without surrender isn't peace, it's prison. Faith says, "You can let go now." Psychology says, "Your nervous system will thank you." Both are right.

We love vulnerability in others but fear it in ourselves. We cheer for authenticity on TED stages but panic when it leaks out mid-Zoom call. We want to look brave but not *be* brave. But confidence isn't the absence of fear, it's the presence of warmth. And warmth without strength feels unstable, while strength without warmth feels unapproachable. The magic is in the mix. The most divine thing you can be is deeply, undeniably human.

People call empathy a "soft skill," but that's hilarious. Empathy is hardly "soft"! Quite the contrary—from my experience, it's a full-contact sport. Google's Project Aristotle proved that teams with high psychological safety—teams where people felt safe being real—outperformed teams where people had the highest IQs. Emotional safety builds results spreadsheets can't. You can teach skill, but you can't fake safety. Your humanity *is* your competitive advantage.

I learned that when my armor finally broke mid-keynote. Perfect slides, confident pacing, audience nodding...and suddenly my brain bluescreened. Total system crash. For five eternal seconds, I stared at the crowd, every neuron yelling at me, "Fake a fainting spell!" Instead, I said, "Wow...my brain just resigned mid-sentence."

The room laughed, not politely, but like people who'd been waiting for permission to exhale. That was the moment I stopped performing confidence and started *becoming* it. That was also the moment when I learned an important lesson: authenticity doesn't weaken your message, it *is* the message. Pretending is exhausting. "Fine" is emotional beige: safe but soulless.

Your nervous system relaxes when your words finally match your truth. That's coherence, the opposite of burnout. Faith says, "Be still." Psychology says, "Regulate." Turns out, they're preaching the same sermon. The performance drains you. Honesty recharges you. Peace doesn't come from being bulletproof, it comes from putting the bullets down.

Here's the truth: although that armor served you once—it got you through storms you didn't deserve to survive—strength isn't how long you can carry that armor, it's knowing when to set it down. When the armor gets heavy, that's not failure. That's evolution. It's God whispering, "You don't need that anymore." So, breathe. Loosen the straps. Let it fall. The world doesn't need more people pretending to be strong, it needs more people strong enough to be real.

The L.I.G.H.T. Model™ Framework

One of my favorite frameworks is The L.I.G.H.T. Model™. (Yes, there's an acronym—don't act surprised!) It goes:

- **L**isten
- **I**nvite
- **G**round
- **H**umor
- **T**ell the Truth

Presence is power. Curiosity creates safety. Regulation restores clarity. Humor heals when it's honest. And when spoken kindly, truth bridges fear faster than any strategy deck ever could. So, lighten up. Literally! Because when your soul gets oxygen, your leadership gets traction.

> **WITHIN REACH TOOLKIT**
> *The Light Gets In*

1. The check-engine soul test.

If your peace feels off, don't ignore it! Your warning lights might sound like:

- "I'm fine" on repeat.
- Constant fatigue, even after rest.
- Joy that feels muted.
- A weird sense of distance from yourself.

Any or all of those might be signs that you're experiencing emotional dysregulation, or put differently, a nudge to pray differently. Either way, pull over. Don't pop the hood alone!

2. The vulnerability ladder.

Don't start with trauma; start with truth.

- Level 1: "Honestly, I'm nervous."
- Level 2: "That feedback hit harder than I had expected."

- Level 3: "I'm afraid I'm letting people down."
- Level 4: "Here's why I built that wall."

Climb slowly. The goal isn't exposure, it's alignment.

3. The LIGHT Model™ revisited:

- Listen: Stop rehearsing your next line; hear their real one.
- Invite: Ask, "How are you, really?" and mean it.
- Ground: Breathe before you speak.
- Humor: Laugh to connect, not to hide.
- Tell the truth: Say the hard things kindly.

Faith translation: Speak the truth in love, Ephesians 4:15.

4. The Faith x Psychology equation.

While faith says "Be still" and psychology says "Regulate," both really mean "Stop running from what hurts long enough to let it heal." Remember: God's strength doesn't require your performance, just your permission.

5. Reflection prompt: setting down the armor

Ask yourself:

- What am I carrying that God never asked me to?
- Who have I become to survive what broke me?
- What would happen if I believed that being seen was safer than being strong?

Write it. Pray it. Later, laugh about it. For now, though, just breathe. Because the light isn't trying to find you—it's just been waiting for you to open the door.

The Reachable Moment

Eventually, every season of carrying catches up to you. The armor that once protected you becomes evidence of how long you've been at war. And when that moment comes, when the weight stops protecting and starts crushing, you remember something sacred: God never asked you to be bulletproof, He just asked you to believe. Strength was never the goal. Surrender was.

Peace doesn't mean the battle's over, it means you've stopped fighting yourself. Maybe the distance between who you are and who you're meant to be was never as far as it felt—maybe it was always within reach.

Within Reach After All

When I first thought about writing this book, my brain's immediate reaction was, "This is going to take forever." After all, I'm not an author, or at least I wasn't before I started this project. I didn't have a clue how the half-formed ideas bouncing around my skull were supposed to turn from mental mush into something meaningful. I figured authors had some kind of magical ritual involving a cabin, a typewriter, and a caffeine IV drip. Then, BOOM! There it was: the reminder I didn't know I needed.

I've never had anything "figured out." Details have never been my strong suit. My memory is decent only when it comes to early 2000s rap lyrics. If you need someone to recite "Ride Wit Me" by Nelly or "Lose Yourself" by Eminem, word for word, I'm your guy. But remembering where I put my wallet or phone? Forget it.

So, no, I didn't plan this book. But apparently, God did. Two of my friends, Ryan, and Trebor, each told me within a day of each other that I should write a book. Neither of them knew the other had said it. And I hadn't seen either of them in ages. That's what I call a God Moment, when the universe taps you on the shoulder twice because it knows you didn't listen the first time. So, I said yes. Not because I knew how, but because something in me whispered, "Do it anyway."

Flow State, Faith State

When I started typing, it felt like a dam was breaking. Every thought, every story, every lesson that had been simmering for years finally burst through. It wasn't strategy, and it wasn't discipline, either. It was flow, that psychological sweet spot where your brain, heart, and purpose align.

Psychologists call it transcendent absorption. I call it "typing so fast I thought my keyboard was about to file a complaint."

And somehow...one chapter became two. Then ten. Then twenty-two. Ninety percent of it poured out over 20 days. No ghostwriter, no outline, just divine caffeine and blind faith. That's not coincidence, that's calling. Still, though, as I write this final chapter, the fear keeps showing up like that one friend who says, "I'm five minutes away" but hasn't even left the house. What if they don't like it? I kept wondering. What if no one reads it? What if I just spent a year writing something that gets three likes and a sympathy repost from my mom?

That voice—the inner critic we all have—loves to show up at the finish line. But here's the psychology behind it: fear isn't a stop sign, it's a signal. It means your brain recognizes meaning. It means you care. So instead of deleting everything, I listened to that fear...and kept typing anyway. Because I know I'm not special—I'm not the first to overthink my potential or question my worth. If I feel like this, chances are you do, too. And if I can write something that helps someone else get a little closer to their dream, then it's not just writing, it's purpose work.

And so now we're here, at the very end—you, me, and this book. We've been through a lot together: the doubt, the stories, the laughter, the "Did he really just quote Eminem in a (not a) self-help book?" moments. And it all comes down to one question: What's next?

We each have different stories, backgrounds, advantages, and battles. But the challenge is universal: How will you live your purpose, maximize your potential, and find your gold?

That question is the great equalizer. It doesn't care about your GPA, your zip code, or your LinkedIn endorsements. It only cares about your willingness to reach. One of my favorite quotes is from Ayn Rand's *Atlas Shrugged*: "Do not let your fire go out, spark by irreplaceable spark, in the hopeless swamps of the not-quite, the not-yet, and the not-at-all. Do not let the hero in your soul perish in lonely frustration for the life you deserved and have never been able to reach. The world you desire can be won. It exists. It is real. It is possible. It's yours." You can almost hear her say, "It's within reach," can't you?

This book wouldn't exist without the thinkers, teachers, and truth-tellers who paved the way, people like Ayn Rand, Simon Sinek, Malcolm Gladwell, Alex Hormozi, and, of course, Jesus. Their words reached me when I needed them most. My only goal was to pass that reach along to you. If even 1% of what I wrote hits you where it matters, then I've done my job. My job is to ignite—I want to use every ounce of what God gave me. I want to leave nothing in the tank. And when I finally meet Him, I pray He says, "Well done, good and faithful servant."

But until then, I'm not done yet. Not even close. And neither are you! You. Aren't. Doing. Enough. Not because you're failing, but because you're capable of more than you think. And you have more inside of you waiting to be utilized! You just have to reach within. Action is the great equalizer, yet it's the thing most people fail to do because they're busy planning to do as opposed to actually doing.

Let's make a deal: let's collectively agree to take action and fulfill our purpose, one reach at a time. Let's light up the world, one spark at a time. That gap between who you are and who you're meant to be? It's not miles wide. It's just a stretch of belief, courage, and small daily steps. And that distance is within reach.

The Real Authors of This Book

Here's the unfiltered truth: Nobody accomplishes anything meaningful alone. Not Arnold, not Ironman, not even the Chick-fil-A drive-thru team (and those people are basically Navy SEALs with polo shirts). This book may have my name on the cover, but it was built on the shoulders, pages, and out-of-my-league genius of people far greater than me: Malcolm Gladwell, Dale Carnegie, James Allen, and Simon Sinek, the Mount Rushmore of "Hey John, maybe try being a better human." Their books are the required reading for anyone who's ever had a dream, a doubt, or a deadline.

To my kids: Noah, Brielle, and Nicholas. You three are the greatest plot twists, purpose, and proof of God's generosity I'll ever have. You're my oxygen, my why, and occasionally the reason I consider noise-canceling headphones a tax write-off. Everything I do, I do so you can proudly say, "See that guy over there who won't stop talking? Yeah... That's my dad." I pray these pages help you understand me better one day, and I hope that by watching Daddy choose the hard, on purpose, you'll learn to do the same. Remember: "Easy training, hard war; hard training, easy war." Always choose hard, unless it's laundry. Then choose delegation.

To my parents. Thank you for the life, the love, and the lessons, especially the one where you somehow managed to convince a kid from Mineral Ridge that he could belong in rooms he'd never seen before. I'd give anything for one more hug, one more conversation, one more chance to say, "Hey, all the stuff you poured into me? It worked!" Some days, I know I make you proud. Other days, I imagine you both leaning over Heaven's balcony like, "Thank God he's pretty." Or "He's *trying.*" But I'm evolving. Slowly, like a Windows update. And I hope you see the man you always prayed I'd become taking shape. I miss you both more than I could ever say and I can't wait for our reunion.

To Javier Lopera, Jason Didion, and Ozan Ozkan, my Toledo Trio. My brothers-from-other-mothers whom time and distance tried to separate but failed. We've known each other longer than half the people reading this have been alive. And even when years go by without seeing each other, we pick up like it's been five minutes. True friendship breaks all laws of time and space, especially Newton's laws, which I'm convinced he made up just to get some attention.

To Joe Manganiello, Alex Rodriguez, and Ryan Weirich. The Los Angeles Trio doesn't have a cool nickname yet, but the loyalty is unmatched. I've leaned on each of you through seasons when I desperately needed people who were steady, honest, and present. I'm extremely proud and grateful to have you in my inner circle. I wouldn't be this healthy—physically, mentally, or emotionally—without you. Thank you.

To the people I get to call friends. Ross, Rachel, Joey, Chandler, Monica, Phoebe... My mistake! Wrong friends. To *my* friends, the real ones who helped shape the guy typing these words, thank you. We are all the sum of our inner circle, and I somehow hit the jackpot, the Powerball, *and* Publisher's Clearing House all at once. You've inspired me more than you'll ever know.

To Tim Buchanan. You were my first friend, and honestly, man...it was rough. You were better at every sport, making it nearly impossible for any girl within a five-mile radius to notice I existed. So, thank you, sincerely, for making it clear early in life that athletics was not going to be my golden ticket. You indirectly shoved me toward academics, ambition, hustle, and eventually this book. That's a real friend.

To Jim Evans. For most of middle and high school, we were functionally the same person: same jokes, same adventures, same questionable decisions. Our mall cruises, parking lot hangs, and baseball days will forever be core memories. I still don't know which stories are yours or mine—that's the beauty of the friendship we had.

To Bobby Bako and Jason Grove. Let's be honest: I was the third coolest guy out of the three of us. You two carried the cool for our senior year Escapades skit and dragged me, willingly, out of not-cool purgatory for one glorious, unforgettable week. I'll never hear "What is love?" ever again and *not* think of the two of you. That skit gave me the faux confidence I needed to march into Toledo like I had a clue who I was. That fake confidence turned into real discovery. Thank you.

To mentees, colleagues, students, and people who shared their stories with me. You are the heartbeat of this book. Every chapter is stitched together from lessons I learned alongside you. You taught me far more than I ever taught you, and I say that as someone who lectures people professionally. Thank you for letting me learn from your lives and thank you for trusting me to speak any form of thoughts, advice, dare I say, wisdom. Your belief in me as a voice in your life is humbling and an honor I take very seriously.

To Trebor Jacquez, principal in the Los Angeles Unified School District. You were the one who lit the spark and gave me the idea to write this book. You have been a believer in me since I met you, and I greatly appreciate your support and encouragement. Know that this book wouldn't be happening without you. Thank you.

To Marla Uliana, Dean at Los Angeles Mission College. You're living proof that leadership can be brilliant, kind, and slightly terrifying in its accuracy. You validated my ideas before they were ideas. You saw something worth pursuing long before I ever believed I could write something worth reading. Without that early encouragement, this book might still be an abandoned Google Doc buried under a pile of grocery lists and half-written rants.

To Alex Hermozi. If Peter Drucker is the Father of Modern Management, you should be named the Godfather of Modern Business. The amount of useful, cool, interesting things I've learned through your books, videos, and podcasts is astounding. You are doing revolutionary things in this world, and we are all better off because of you. Thank you for your wisdom, encouragement, and guidance from a distance.

To caffeine. Beloved. Faithful. Overly enabling. You have been my most stable adult relationship. I don't know if that's inspiring or mildly alarming, but here we are. If the *Guinness Book of World Records* had a category for "Most cups consumed while chasing a dream," I'd like to think I'd be competitive.

To the person reading this. Yes, *you.* Thank you for trusting me with your time, the most precious currency in existence (right behind Taylor Swift tickets). My hope is that this book moves you a little closer to the person you're meant to become. And please remember: *you're closer than you think.*

And finally, Jesus. My first encourager, my loudest cheerleader, and the One who whispered this dream into my spirit more than a decade ago. Thank you for opening doors I didn't know existed, for using my mess as raw material for purpose, and for reminding me daily that nobody can out-fail Your grace. Thank you for loving me relentlessly, forgiving me repeatedly, and guiding me patiently. Anything good in this book came from You.

Please Note: If you're reading this right now and are thinking to yourself, *I would like to have a relationship with Jesus*, well, you're in luck! We're actually offering a free relationship with Jesus with every purchase of this book! All you have to do is recite the following words and believe them in your heart:

Heavenly Father, I come to You in the name of Jesus. I know that I am a sinner and need Your forgiveness. I believe that Jesus is Your Son, that He died for my sins, and that You raised Him from the dead. I turn from my sins and open the door of my heart and life to You. I accept Jesus as my personal Lord and Savior. Thank You for forgiving my sins and giving me eternal life. Take control of my life and make me the kind of person You want me to be. In Jesus' name, Amen.

Like I said before, everything you want
in this life is within reach. Especially Jesus.

...and the Movement

John Kundly is a leadership coach, keynote speaker, and career influencer who built a life, and a message, around the sacred idea that nothing is wasted. Not the detours. Not the doubts. Not the Tuesday afternoons that feel like background noise until God taps your shoulder and says, *"Pay attention... this part matters."* He firmly believes every life is one brave reach away from becoming something incredible.

As the founder of **Reach With John,** creator of **@reachwithjohn,** and author of *Within Reach,* John helps ambitious, overthinking professionals bridge the gap between who they *are* and who they're *called to become.* His voice blends God and faith, behavioral neuroscience, hard-earned experience, and comedic honesty forged through a lifetime of unexpected plot twists.

Before launching his speaking and coaching platform and becoming one of the most trusted voices in modern career development, John spent the last two decades leading teams spanning utilities, media & entertainment, and engineering consulting. As an Executive of multiple billion dollar companies, he proved that people-first leadership isn't soft, it's strategic, scalable, and wildly profitable.

His spark didn't come from a boardroom, it came from a retail shift at Express, a Monday night in Omaha, and a series of divine "are you kidding me?" moments along the way.

Today, John blends real-world experience, faith, and psychology to create content and talks that are equal parts education and stand-up. His mission is simple: to help people bridge the gap between who they *are* and who they're *meant to be.* Whether he's on stage, on TikTok, or in a boardroom full of executives, his message stays the same—**growth doesn't happen in leaps; it happens in reach.**

Aspiring professionals encounter John's message across social media, conferences, classrooms, and corporate workshops. His frameworks help people unlock purpose, confidence, and communication skills rooted in behavioral science and anchored in faith.

John lives in Southern California, where he divides his time between being a dad to his three amazing children, writing, speaking, and mentoring young professionals, all while testing the limits of how much coffee one man can safely consume in a day.